From Cricket to Christ

From Cricket to Christ

C.T. Studd

David Luckman

CF4KIDS

Copyright © 2025 David Luckman

paperback ISBN 978-1-5271-1215-5
ebook ISBN 978-1-5271-1335-0

Published by
Christian Focus Publications,
Geanies House, Fearn, Tain, Ross-shire,
IV20 1TW, Scotland, U.K.
www.christianfocus.com

Cover design by Daniel van Straaten
Cover illustration by Daniel van Straaten

Printed and bound in Denmark
by Nørhaven

Scripture quotations are from The Holy Bible, English Standard Version, copyright © 2001 by Crossway Bibles, a publishing ministry of Good News Publishers. Used by permission. All rights reserved. esv Text Edition: 2011.

All rights reserved. No part of this publication may be reproduced, stored in a retrieval system, or transmitted, in any form, by any means, electronic, mechanical, photocopying, recording or otherwise without the prior permission of the publisher or a licence permitting restricted copying. In the U.K. such licences are issued by the Copyright Licensing Agency, 4 Battlebridge, London, SE1 2HX www.cla.co.uk

Contents

A Daring Rescue 7

The Years of Change........................ 15

A Clear Mind 27

The Mission to China 37

A Great Giveaway 47

Meeting Priscilla 57

No Foreign Devils Here! 67

The Mission to India 79

Cannibals Want Missionaries 91

Journey to the Heart of Africa 101

The Mission in Africa 107

Bwana Mukubwa 117

C.T. Studd: Timeline 128

Thinking Further 131

A Daring Rescue

C.T. Studd sat on the veranda of his austere home in the heart of Africa having an evening cup of tea with a group of missionaries. Two watchmen, armed with spears, hurriedly approached them with some dreadful news. C.T. stood as they drew near.

'Bwana Mukubwa[1], one of the girls from the school has been taken!' declared a watchman breathlessly.

'Who has taken her?' asked C.T. calmly although he was shocked by the announcement. The others on the veranda stood up quickly at the dreadful news. Edith Buxton, C.T.'s daughter, put her hand over her mouth in shock. Her husband Alfred gently took her other hand by her side in solidarity with her.

'Chief Abiangama. He caught the girl on her way back from school,' said the other watchman.

'He has kept her prisoner,' continued the first watchman.

'Have you tried to get her back?' asked Edith sharply.

'We have already been to the village to demand her back, but the chief will not let her go,' replied the other watchman.

---

1. **Bwana Mukubwa** means "Great White Chief". It was the name given to C.T. Studd by the local tribespeople.

From Cricket to Christ

C.T. knew exactly what to do. 'Go to the centre of the village and raise the alarm,' he commanded the watchmen. They left quickly to carry out their instructions. Edith looked at her father who was lit up in the strong moonlight. She knew that expression on his face. She'd seen it before as they were growing up. There was no doubt that her father would step up and do everything he could to get the girl back safely. It was a rescue mission.

Soon the Christians of the village appeared from the thick palm groves. They picked up anything on their way that could be used to defend themselves. Some carried big sticks, others had *pangas*[2], while the rest had long-handled rakes or hoes that were generally used for weeding.

The crowd gathered at the foot of the steps that led to C.T.'s house. Edith did a quick head count. There were fifty of them. C.T. moved to the top of the steps to address the zealous multitude that stood raucously before him. He raised his hands to beckon for silence. An immediate hush came over them.

'Thank you for your willingness to join in the rescue,' he began. 'It is so deeply encouraging to see your love for your neighbour such that you are willing to risk yourselves for another's wellbeing. But I want this rescue mission to be conducted in a way that pleases our Lord Jesus Christ. So, I want you all to put your

---

2. A **panga** is an African knife which is long, wooden, and used for cultivating crops.

weapons on the ground. We shall rescue the girl as Christians and not as soldiers.'

A murmur of disappointment was heard from the crowd; however, they would obey Bwana Mukubwa. Each rescuer stepped forward and laid their arms in a large pile at the foot of the veranda steps.

'Father's been suffering from fever again, Alfred,' Edith said quietly as the people were disarming themselves. 'He'll need help to get through the jungle.'

'I'll see to it that his hammock is brought out, and I'll pick four strong men to carry it,' replied Alfred.

Hammocks were an important means of transportation for Europeans living in the interior of Africa during the early part of the twentieth century. A travel hammock was a bed of canvas or netting that was attached to a pole at both ends. Travelling by hammock was a status symbol for the wealthy and was often used by African chiefs too.

C.T. never thought of himself as greater than anyone else, except on a cricket field perhaps! He much preferred to travel using his own legs or even his bicycle. But when he was weak with fever, which was a reoccurring problem for him, members of his Christian family in Africa would gladly carry him in his hammock.

The trek through the dense jungle was arduous and sweaty that evening. They heard beating drums and the guttural shouts of dancers long before they got to Chief Abiangama's village. It took the rescue party about an

From Cricket to Christ

hour before they reached the edge of the village. On their approach, they saw about two hundred dancing men with feathers in their hair, swaying rhythmically to the beating of the drums. They stopped in their tracks to discuss their next move.

Albert stood beside C.T.'s hammock and bent down. 'What shall we do, Bwana?' he whispered.

'We shall get the child back,' C.T. replied softly. Then in a firm voice, he commanded his men: 'Break through the circle!'

The rescuers emerged from the jungle and marched firmly through the circle of dancing men, walking right up to Chief Abiangama, before stopping. C.T. jumped out of his hammock and squared off in front of the Chief.

Suddenly C.T. grabbed Chief Abiangama by his beard. 'Where is the girl?!' he demanded, yanking the captured beard in his hand. 'You took her!' Another yank. 'I demand you return her to us!' Yank, yank, yank.

Chief Abiangama quickly pulled away from Bwana Mukubwa, declaring, 'I'll fetch her! I'll fetch her!' grasping his tortured beard as he moved. He quickly ran for cover among his village huts. C.T. followed him in hot pursuit, determined not to be taken in by the words of this scoundrel. His merry band of rescuers were firmly on his tail.

The Chief dodged between the huts, and his many wives, trying to get away. C.T. cut him off at every turn.

C.T. Studd

By now the dancing men were getting involved in the debacle, and armed themselves for an unfair fight. '*Bunduki!*' cried one of the rescuers, which was the *Bangala*[3] word meaning 'guns!' They were everywhere! As emotions ran high, the unarmed rescuers decided to strike first before any shots were fired and someone was killed.

Thud! The bare fists of the rescuers connected with the bodies of their enemies. Edith shrieked. She had never heard so much thumping and pounding. But she knew that sounds always seemed louder in the darkness. All Edith could see was the warriors' feathers bobbing up and down in the moonlight and the flying shirttales of the rescuers as the men and women laid into each other. She made her way back to her father. C.T. looked bewildered by it all.

'How are we going to get out of this, Father?'

'Our fifty rescuers are no match for two hundred warriors, that's for sure.'

Edith had a mad but brilliant idea.

'Father, I'm going to sing.'

Edith had a very high-pitched voice, so there was no way her tune would not be heard. She took a deep breath and began in perfect Bangala:

'Jesus loves me! this I know,
For the Bible tells me so;
Little ones to him belong,
They are weak but he is strong.'

---

3. **Bangala** was the local language of these tribes in the Belgian Congo.

From Cricket to Christ

It was the first song that Edith had learned as a child, and the first song that was translated into the Bangala language.

The tune carried loudly through the village. One by one, the voices of the rescuers joined in. Soon it was a beautiful, melodious chorus that replaced the thuds of fear and self-preservation, and the fighting slowly stopped. How wonderful!

As the brawl died down, one of the chief's wives crawled on all fours through the mass of legs until she silently arrived at C.T.'s side. Like a flash she took his little finger in her mouth, biting down hard so that C.T. let out a loud yell. Heads turned in his direction to see what was happening.

Noticing that it was the chief's wife now causing all the trouble, Edith instinctively protected her father. Momentarily forgetting C.T.'s call not to hurt anyone – just like the other members of C.T.'s rescue party it seemed – she pushed the chief's wife hard, sending her flying through the air and landing on the ground.

There was a lull in the fighting, and C.T. seized the opportunity to call a halt to the whole debacle. He drew a line in the dust with his foot and called the rescuers to come to his side, leaving the chief's warriors on the other. Both groups looked rather more ruffled than they did when C.T.'s group arrived. Then the rescuers marched off back to Nala, singing hymns as they went.

C.T. Studd

'What about the girl?' whispered Albert into C.T.'s ear when they were clear of the village.

'We'll have to try again tomorrow,' replied C.T.

An hour later the weary rescuers arrived back in Nala. To everyone's surprise and joy, the kidnapped girl was sitting on the steps of C.T.'s veranda.

'You're here!' shrieked Edith, running forward to give her a hug. 'When did you get back? How did you escape?!' The rest of the rescue party gathered around her, thrilled she was home safely.

The girl smiled. 'When I heard your voices, and that you had all come for me, I praised God. I knew it was time for me to go home. Then I heard you fight for me.' Tears of joy and love began to trickle down her cheeks. Edith gently wiped them away with her hand.

C.T. gently chastised his rescuers. 'Yes! What part of "no fighting" did you not understand?' They hung their heads, not noticing C.T's wink at Edith, who grinned from ear to ear.

A massive cheer of delight rang out in Nala that night. As the men and women drifted homeward through palm trees, their way illuminated by soft moonlight, Alfred, Edith, and C.T. gathered once again on the veranda.

'When you were growing up in London, did you ever think you'd be chasing down a cannibalistic African Chief to save one of our schoolchildren?' C.T. asked light-heartedly.

From Cricket to Christ

'Oh, not at all!' laughed Edith. 'Can you imagine the look on Granny's face if she were alive to hear what we got up to tonight?'

They could imagine Granny's horrified expression rightly, and the three roared with laughter.

The Years of Change

'When Moody comes to London, I'm going to go hear him,' announced Edward to his wife, Dora, as he threw his newspaper down on the table. 'There must be something good about the man,' Edward went on, 'Or he would never be abused so much by the papers.'

Dwight Lyman Moody, also known as D.L. Moody, was an American evangelist. He was immensely gifted at telling people the gospel of Jesus Christ. He always spoke the truth about Jesus with clarity and passion.

In 1877 Dwight Moody was travelling around the British Isles with his friend and vocalist, Ira Sankey. Together they held meetings in various buildings and halls that could accommodate the growing number of people who would gather to hear Moody proclaim the gospel and Sankey sing hymns.

The way that Moody told the good news about Jesus was fascinating to the British crowds. He spoke plainly and pointedly – the gospel message loosed like an arrow into the hearts and minds of hearers. English clergy didn't seem to preach that way. What is more, Sankey

From Cricket to Christ

sang beautifully worded and pleasantly melodious hymns about Christ Jesus, which were new to the British churchgoer. Sankey had such a lovely voice.

The English newspapers, however, were not so enamoured with the Americans. Moody did not hold the clerical title of 'Reverend', nor did he wear preaching bands around his neck; therefore in their minds, he lacked authenticity. The papers were of the opinion that only the clergy had the authority to engage in such religious activities, and in England they usually did their religious thing on Sundays. But Moody and Sankey held their 'missions' on any evening during the week.

Journalists spoke disparagingly about the Moody and Sankey revival meetings. They even misrepresented the Americans as salesmen – Moody of hymn-books and Sankey of organs.

'Any news from the boys?' asked Edward.

'Nothing today,' Dora replied.

'Ok. I'm going to the study. I have a few letters to write.' Edward left Dora to her thoughts about the boys.

The three eldest Studd boys, Kynaston, George, and C.T., were boarding at Eton, a private school for boys in the ancient and charming village of Windsor in the south-east of England.

Cricket was their passion. They lived and breathed the sport and they were each exceptionally talented. Of the three, C.T. was the most gifted all-rounder. The year that Moody and Sankey toured the British Isles was the only time that all three Studd boys played on the Eton XI[1] together. Edward and Dora were exceptionally proud of the lads for this achievement.

The years passed by quietly for the Studd family as they enjoyed the routines of hunting in the winter and cricket in the summer. Edward had a superb cricket pitch constructed on a huge flat area of grass at the back of the house. It was not unusual for Dora to find her garden neglected because the gardeners were regularly whisked away to make up the numbers for a game of cricket.

Edward also loved horses. He had stables built for the growing number of magnificent studs and mares in his keep. Five of his horses ran in the Grand National, the most prestigious horse race in England. One of them even won it back in 1866. Naturally the children learned to ride horses at an early age. It was important for the Studds to be good horse riders, especially for the hunting season.

Edward loved to visit a leading auctioneer for horses known as Tattersalls, based in Newmarket in the rustic county of West Suffolk, in England. Due to the frequency of his trips to Tattersalls, he decided to buy a townhouse in London's Hyde Park Gardens. It was house number two, and it was an exquisite Victorian mansion situated on the north side of the park. This is where Edward's life changed.

---

1. Eton XI is the name of the school's cricket team. XI are Roman numerals for the number eleven, which is the number of players on a cricket team

From Cricket to Christ

Sitting in his study, behind a beautifully crafted Chippendale desk, Edward wrote to his friend, Mr Vincent, encouraging him to bet money on one of his horses that was competing in an upcoming race. Edward was convinced the horse would win: it was a real beauty. He posted the letter to Mr Vincent the next day, confident his friend would thank him for the wise and lucrative advice.

Shortly after, Edward met Mr Vincent in London and together they drove by carriage to Tattersalls.

'How much money did you put on my horse?' asked Edward.

'None,' said Mr Vincent sheepishly.

'Well, you're the biggest fool I ever saw!' exclaimed Edward, exasperated by the revelation. 'Didn't I tell you what a good horse he was?'

'Yes, Edward, you did.'

It took a moment for the shock to wear off. Edward really thought his advice was sound. Why did Vincent not take it? he wondered.

'Though you are a fool, come and dine with me. The family are all in the country,' Edward said perkily, lifting the tense atmosphere in the car.

Later that afternoon, the Tattersalls business was concluded, and the men headed back to the Hyde Park townhouse for a sumptuous dinner – just what was needed after a hard day at the auctioneers.

As they quietly shared an after-dinner digestif, Edward broke the silence abruptly, saying, 'Where shall we go to amuse ourselves? I'll go anywhere you suggest.'

'How about Drury Lane?' Vincent said, knowing that Moody and Sankey had arrived in London and were having meetings at the Theatre Royal.

'What? Isn't that where those fellows Moody and Sankey are? The papers have been full of them, and I mean to hear them but, for a start, today is not Sunday. Let's go to the theatre or a concert instead?' responded Edward, hoping that his friend would change his mind.

'Now, you are a man of your word, Edward, and you said you would go where I chose. I choose Drury Lane.' Mr Vincent was gently determined in his reply, because something wonderful had happened to him on a recent trip to Ireland.

Mr Vincent had heard Dwight Moody proclaim the gospel of Christ in a theatre in Dublin, and he became a Christian. Mr Vincent was hopeful that his dear friend, Mr Edward Studd, would do the same.

'Ok,' agreed Edward. 'Let's go to Drury Lane, and hear the good Messrs Moody and Sankey.'

The theatre at Drury Lane was packed with people. There didn't seem to be any more room for Mr Vincent and Edward when they arrived. Determined that Edward should hear the gospel from Moody, Mr Vincent began to work his way through the crowd on the street until he found a member of the organising committee.

'Look, here. I have a wealthy sporting friend with me. I will never get him here again if you don't get us

From Cricket to Christ

seats tonight,' said Mr Vincent loudly over the din of the crowd.

Edward and Mr Vincent were led through a green door to a couple of empty seats right in front of the stage. After the opening songs, Dwight Moody addressed the attentive throng, speaking plainly the gospel of Christ. Edward Studd never took his eyes of Mr Moody until he had finished speaking. Throughout the proceedings Mr Vincent prayed in the quietness of his own mind that God would open the blind eyes of his friend, so that he would repent and trust in Jesus.

After the meeting was over, Mr Vincent looked his friend in the eye. 'Well, what did you think of that?' he asked Edward.

'I will come and hear this man again. He just told me everything I had ever done!' he replied astonished.

While Moody and Sankey were in London, Edward kept going to hear them until he was fully convicted of his sin, repented, turning to Christ as his Saviour and Lord. His life changed drastically from that moment. He was no longer interested in the things that used to give him pleasure, things like horse racing, or resplendent dances, or playing cards. Instead, he wanted his sons to know Christ personally and to be saved.

Kynaston, George, and Charles were unaware of the change that happened to their father because they were away studying at Eton. Then one day they received a letter from their father asking if the boys could meet him in London. They wondered if he was going to take them to a show. It wasn't until they met him at number two Hyde Park Gardens that his plan was revealed.

'A God Talk!' exclaimed C.T. to his equally disappointed brothers. They were upstairs in his bedroom, discussing their father's plans and being careful not to be too loud for fear that his father might hear and reprove him.

'It's not even Sunday,' added George in exasperation. 'What's happened to father?'

'Isn't it obvious? He's got religion!' C.T. blurted out. George put his head in his hands.

'Come on, we'd better go down now, or we'll be late,' said Kynaston, 'And you know that father doesn't like tardiness.'

Edward's dutiful boys piled into the carriage, and off they set for Drury Lane. Edward's face was beaming with excitement because he knew what was coming that evening. His eldest sons would hear the gospel of Christ clearly and passionately, perhaps for the first time in their lives. Edward's heart yearned for all his children to know the mercy and grace of the Lord Jesus for themselves.

C.T. found the address interesting enough. Mr Moody was certainly passionate in the delivery of his talk concerning Jesus Christ, the Son of God. Yet C.T. and his brothers hardened their hearts to the gospel that day.

Over the course of the year, Edward took his sons to hear other men who preached the Word of God.

From Cricket to Christ

He even opened the large hall of Tedworth House, his luxurious home in Wiltshire, to host gospel meetings, inviting many speakers to come and share the good news of Christ with his friends. People travelled from all over England to attend these gatherings; C.T. saw many of them convert to Christ.

It wasn't until one weekend in the summer of 1877, when Kynaston, George, and C.T. were home from Eton, that the brothers' lives were ineffably changed. Edward had invited two men to come to Tedworth House and preach the gospel. One was likeable enough, but the other was thought to be indecisive and weak by the older boys. His name was Mr Weatherby, and he was certainly worthy to have a trick played on him.

When, in general chit-chat, Mr Weatherby divulged that he could ride a horse, the boys seized the moment and invited him to go for a morning ride with them and their father.

'Of course, but I should warn you that I am not a very accomplished horseman,' Mr Weatherby confessed.

Perfect, thought C.T. as a mischievous plan developed in his mind.

Mr Weatherby and Mr Studd rode gently out of the stables in front of the boys. When they had ridden for a while across the open fields surrounding Tedworth House, the three brothers looked at each other and a rascally smirk came across their faces. One by one they roused their horses and galloped like the wind past the two men. Nothing could hold the men's horses from cantering after the exuberant tricksters. Mr Weatherby held on to the reigns for dear life as the boys raced ahead, enjoying every moment of his obvious discomfort.

Throughout the ride, the boys performed their impish trick on Mr Weatherby a few times more. Even Edward chuckled at the comical sight of Mr Weatherby being thrown this way and that in the saddle. Much to their surprise, however, Mr Weatherby remained on the back of the horse. Clearly he had more grit than the Studds had given him credit for.

Later that afternoon, it was Mr Weatherby's turn to engage in an activity that he was gifted in – talking to people about the Lord Jesus Christ. One by one, he took each boy aside to a quiet corner of Tedworth House and challenged them to turn to Christ as Saviour and Lord and live their lives for Jesus.

'Where are you off to, young Charles?' asked Mr Weatherby jovially. C.T. was dressed in his cricket gear; it was plain to him, indeed to the whole world, where he was going.

'The cricket field,' C.T. replied pleasantly, as he stopped to speak with old Weatherby just for a moment.

'Yes, I hear you are a dab hand at cricket!' smiled Mr Weatherby. C.T. nodded. 'So tell me, C.T., are you a Christian?'

From Cricket to Christ

The question took C.T. completely by surprise. One moment they were amicably talking about cricket, and now old Weatherby wanted to talk about Jesus!

'I am not what you call a Christian, Mr Weatherby. I have believed in Jesus Christ since I was knee high.' C.T. cleared his throat and continued, 'Of course I believe in the church too.'

There, that should do him, thought C.T. Perhaps he'll go away and let me get on with my game.

'Look here,' Mr Weatherby shot back, 'God so loved the world, that he gave his only begotten Son, that whosoever believeth in him should not perish, but have everlasting life.[2] You believe Jesus Christ died?'

'Yes,' came the curt reply.

'You believe he died for you?'

'Yes.'

'Do you believe the other half of the verse — that you shall "have everlasting life?"'

'No. I don't believe that.'

'Don't you think that you are a bit inconsistent, believing one half of the verse and not the other half?' asked Mr Weatherby incredulously.

'I suppose I am.'

'Well, are you always going to be inconsistent?' Weatherby was hoping for a negative answer.

'No, I suppose not always.'

Good, thought Weatherby. 'Will you be consistent now?' he asked the young cricketer before him.

---

2. John 3:16.

Mr Weatherby could see the look in C.T.'s eye that suggested the cogs of his young brain were whirring as he tried to think of an answer.

Old Weatherby's backed me into a corner! C.T. thought. *If I go out of this room, I won't carry very much self-respect.*

'Yes. I will be consistent,' C.T. conceded.

'Well, don't you see that eternal life is a gift?' probed Mr Weatherby. 'When somebody gives you a present at Christmas, what do you do?'

'I take it and say, "Thank you," ' C.T. answered.

'Will you say, "Thank you" to God for this gift?'

Without hesitation C.T. dropped to his knees in front of Mr Weatherby, who quickly joined him in a prayer of thanks to God: for his Son, Jesus Christ, who died on the cross for the sins of the whole world, and for the gift of eternal life to all who believe and follow him. Immediately C.T. had an overwhelming sense of God's peace in his soul.

Am I a Christian? Yes! Yes I am! C.T. rejoiced in his heart.[3]

---

3. C.T. Studd's personal testimony can be found in his book *The Fundamentals – A Testimony,* Volume 3 (Testimony Publishing Company, Chicago, 1910), Chapter 3, pages 119-126.

A Clear Mind

After his father died in 1877, C.T. went to Cambridge University to study law. On that wonderful day of his conversion with Mr Weatherby, C.T. acknowledged Christ as Saviour, but he did not truly submit to Christ as Lord. He did little to live out his Christian faith in those years at Cambridge. Instead he threw himself into cricket, and he rose to the top of the cricket world, even though he was still a student and not a full-time professional sportsman. Nonetheless, newspapers and sporting magazines asserted C.T. Studd as one of the greatest cricketers England had ever produced. He was famous and the focus of the nation's adulation.

It wasn't until a serious bout of pneumonia[1] befell his brother George that C.T. was shaken from his spiritual lethargy. George's bedroom was on the third floor at Number Two Hyde Park Gardens, London. Every night C.T. sat at his sick brother's bedside, keeping him company and tending to his fever. There was no hesitation in C.T.'s care of his brother, no fear that he might catch the illness from George's episodes of coughing and spluttering.

---

1. **Pneumonia** is a serious illness caused by severe inflammation of the lungs.

From Cricket to Christ

Sometimes George feverishly tossed and turned under the blankets as the illness did its best to sink him into an early grave. C.T sat in a chair next to the bed and began to ask himself some penetrating questions.

Now, what is all the popularity of the world worth to George? he wondered. What is all the fame and flattery worth? What good is it to possess all the riches in the world when faced with eternity? As C.T. looked helplessly at George, a voice seemed to answer him in his mind, with a phrase from the Bible that said, 'Vanity of vanities ... all is vanity.'[2]

By God's grace, George recovered well over the next number of weeks. C.T. took advantage of his brother's recovery and allowed himself to steal away from George one evening to hear Mr Moody, who was back in London.

'Oh George, it was wonderful!' declared C.T., upon returning to George's bedroom in Hyde Park Gardens. 'And I can feel it.' C.T. was pacing up and down the room as he spoke excitedly to his intrigued brother who was sitting up in bed.

'Feel what, C.T.?' asked George enthusiastically.

'That the Lord has restored to me the joy of his salvation!'

'Praise God indeed!' exclaimed George, as his face lit up with a smile.

---

2. **Ecclesiastes 1:2,** meaning everything this world has to offer us is futile or pointless.

C.T. Studd

'God has a work for me to do, George, and I must do it.'

'Do share,' said George.

'I will dedicate myself to winning souls for the Lord. I will point every man and woman and boy and girl to the Saviour. There is no greater work!'

'Not even hitting a test century for England at the Oval[3]?' jested George.

'Not even that, George,' smiled C.T.

'Marvellous!' cheered George as he punched the air with his fists. 'Where will you start this new work?'

C.T. thought for a brief moment. 'With the people that God has placed in my life who do not know him. What about the cricket squad at Cambridge? I can take them to hear Moody while he's in town.'

'Splendid idea!' affirmed George.

Several of the England cricket team went to hear Moody at C.T.'s behest. A few of them even went on to profess faith in the Lord Jesus Christ. But when Moody's mission in London finished, C.T. was at a loss for what to do next. In his heart he only wanted to serve Christ, but the how and where eluded him. It was at this juncture that he came upon a tract, written anonymously from the pen of an unbeliever which had a surprisingly profound impact on C.T. and jolted him into action for the Master.

---

3. **The Oval** is a famous cricket ground in south London, first opened in 1845.

From Cricket to Christ

The tract read:

'Did I firmly believe, as millions say they do, that the knowledge and practice of religion in this life influences destiny in another, religion would mean everything to me. I would cast away earthly enjoyments as dross, earthly cares as follies, and earthly thoughts and feelings as vanity. Religion would be my first waking thought and my last image before sleep sank me into unconsciousness. I would labour in its cause alone. I would take thought of the morrow of eternity alone. I would esteem one soul gained for heaven worth a life of suffering. Earthly consequences would never stay my hand, nor seal my lips. Earth, its joys and its griefs, would occupy no moment of my thoughts. I would strive to look upon eternity alone, and on the immortal souls around me, soon to be everlasting happy or everlasting miserable. I would go forth to the world and preach to it in season and out of season, and my text would be, WHAT SHALL IT PROFIT A MAN IF HE GAIN THE WHOLE WORLD AND LOSE HIS OWN SOUL?'[4]

Immediately C.T.'s mind was clear. The challenge of the tract helped him realise how inconsistent his Christian life had been up to that point. From now on, he would serve Christ and only Christ. But how? and where? He kept thinking about mission work overseas. Although his family preferred that he should

---

4. C.T. Studd, *Cricketer and Pioneer*, by Norman P. Grubb (The Lutterworth Press, Cambridge, 1933) page 36.

C.T. Studd

stay in England, his heart was breaking for lost sinners in faraway lands.

It was a visit from university friend Stanley Smith in 1884 that helped sharpen the focus of C.T.'s mind on Christian service overseas.

Kynaston and C.T. were at home when Stanley knocked on the door. He received a happy welcome from the men who ushered him in to the drawing room. They settled into some comfortable seats close to the fire.

'I am really glad I caught you both in today,' said Stanley.

'You did well to get us on a Saturday, Stanley. We are usually busy during the day. I'm not out until later this afternoon,' said Kynaston.

'That's a pity. I'm heading into the city for a meeting this evening, and I was going to invite you both.'

'What's the meeting?' asked C.T.

'There's this chap, John McCarthy, you may have heard of him?'

'No,' replied Kynaston. C.T. shook his head.

'Anyway, McCarthy is a missionary with the China Inland Mission, and he's heading back to China. They're having a farewell for him at their headquarters.'

'A missionary in China, is he? That sounds interesting. I'll go with you, Stanley,' C.T. said agreeably.

'Sorry, Stanley, I'll have to pass on this one,' said Kynaston.

'That's alright, Kynaston, old chap. I'm sure there'll be other meetings,' Stanley reassured him.

31

From Cricket to Christ

The China Inland Mission, or C.I.M., was an organisation that wanted to evangelise central China with the gospel of Jesus Christ. It was founded in 1865 by James Hudson Taylor[5] and a number of other like-minded Christians, including John McCarthy.

During the farewell service that evening at the C.I.M. headquarters, Mr McCarthy spoke about his twenty years of ministry in China, and the dire need of gospel missionaries to share the good news of Christ in China.

'There are thousands of souls perishing every day and night without even the knowledge of the Lord Jesus,' revealed Mr McCarthy, his voice breaking with the heartfelt agony of every lost soul's hell-bound eternity.

The thought of all those people headed for an eternity in hell nearly made C.T. stand up and offer himself for the Lord's service in China straightaway. But he remained in his seat, lest anyone should accuse him of acting impulsively in light of Mr McCarthy's emotional address. Instead, C.T. decided that he would pray to his Heavenly Father for guidance.

There was a niggling doubt in his mind about going to China. It revolved around his mother. What would she think of him leaving her and England? It would break her heart if I went to China to be a missionary, he thought.

---

5. For more information, read the Trail Blazer *Hudson Taylor: An Adventure Begins* by Catherine Mackenzie, CF4K, Christian Focus Publications, 2014.

C.T. Studd

C.T. took a little Bible out of his pocket. He flipped through the pages, stopping partway through Matthew's Gospel. He read, 'Whoever loves father or mother more than me is not worthy of me'.[6] It was enough to settle his doubts. C.T. now believed in his heart that God wanted him to go to China.

Soon after he made an appointment to speak with Mr Hudson Taylor, the director of C.I.M. It was a positive meeting and C.T. was accepted as a mission associate of C.I.M. His good friend Stanley Smith, who'd taken him to the farewell service of Mr McCarthy, did the same thing.

In a matter of weeks, five other friends from Cambridge University decided to join them in the adventure. They were given the nickname, 'The Cambridge Seven,' and it wasn't long before the papers got hold of their story – seven young, gifted men from one of England's finest universities were going out to China as missionaries.

The Cambridge Seven were: C.T. Studd, Stanley Smith, Montagu Beauchamp, Arthur Polhill-Turner, Cecil Polhill-Turner, Dixon Hoste, and William Cassells. All of them came from the upper echelons of English society, and each young man was remarkably resilient and athletic. The fact that they were giving everything up to serve Christ in squalor in the heart of China caused a stir to say the least. People were fascinated by this – what would possess a man to give

---

6. Matthew 10:37.

From Cricket to Christ

up wealth and luxury for poverty and hardship in a foreign land amongst people who did not speak the Queen's English? Would anyone in their right mind do such a thing?

The young men began touring the country and speaking to university students about their faith in Christ and their mission to China. People came out in thousands to hear these men, and many were converted to follow Christ. A spiritual revival had broken out in England! Even Victoria, Queen of England, was most pleased to receive a booklet containing the testimonies of The Cambridge Seven.

The time was approaching for the Seven to sail to China and begin their work for the Master there. C.I.M. arranged three great farewell meetings, at the Guildhall in Cambridge, the Corn Exchange in Oxford, and Exeter Hall in London. Each venue was packed out with people keen to hear the men's testimonies and the answer to the question 'Why go to China at all?'

Leading academics invited C.T. and Stanley to speak to their medical students at Edinburgh University in the heart of the capital city of Scotland.

On a bleak December evening, Stanley and C.T. entered the packed hall to a raucous welcome. It was decided that C.T. should address the assembly first. Next would be a returning missionary from China. Last would be Stanley.

Although he was not a good public speaker, the students and professors were captivated by C.T.'s

C.T. Studd

devotion to Jesus Christ. The crowd cheered again and again as they listened to C.T. It was impossible for C.T. to hide how much he loved the Lord.

Stanley was an eloquent speaker. They listened to him in complete silence as he challenged the selfishness of their hearts, and their lack of service in the local churches. The Holy Spirit was working in the hearts and minds of the hearers, convicting them of sin and calling them to bow their knees to Jesus Christ.

When Stanley had finished, the chair of the meeting stood up and said, 'If any of you would like to shake hands with these young men and wish them "Godspeed" on their journey to China, then come forward after I pronounce the benediction.' The expectation was low, that only a few well-wishers would have the courage to approach the guest speakers at the end.

The hall went quiet as God's blessing was pronounced upon all who were there. Once over, there was a mad scramble to the platform! Students jostled each other as they crowded around C.T. and Stanley, genuinely interested to hear more about Jesus Christ and his gospel.

On that cold December night in 1884, the Spirit of Christ was at work in Edinburgh.

The Mission to China

'All aboard!' announced the train conductor from the bustling platform of Victoria Station in London. His words excited the group of people standing outside the door of the carriage in which the Cambridge Seven sat waiting to go to China.

'Make sure you write to us!' their relatives and friends shouted.

'Of course we will,' came the reassuring reply from the open carriage.

The train's whistle blew loudly, declaring, 'We're off!' The doors of the carriages closed quickly and the wheels began to slip on the tracks from the sheer force of pressure produced by the steam-powered engine. Slowly, they found traction and started to pull away from the station. Friends and relatives of all the passengers waved and cheered as many of them escorted the train to the end of the platform. They could see arms and hands vigorously waving from most of the carriage windows in response to their farewells until, finally, the train was out of sight.

For the loved ones of the Cambridge Seven, it hit them – it was real. The young men were truly on their way to China. C.T. watched the green fields of his

From Cricket to Christ

homeland whizz by as the train sped towards the port. It was the 5th of February, 1885. He wondered if he would ever see those green fields again, or would he spend the rest of his life in the heart of China. His life was in the Lord's hands. His will be done, thought C.T.

On board the ship, the young missionaries settled into their sparse accommodation. Almost immediately they began talking to the other passengers and crew about Jesus and his gospel. It was their hearts' desire to see all people walking the straight path to eternal life.

C.T. wrote a letter to his mother telling her all about it:

> There are seven second-class passengers, and we trust that all are now God's own children. The case of one is truly marvellous. The man is a captain of an Indian steamer and had been noted for lying, drunkenness, swearing and blasphemy. Well, thank God, He has brought even this man to know Jesus as his Saviour. Dixon Hoste began to talk to him the first day, then somehow, one afternoon the Lord led me to go and speak to him about his soul. He seemed softened and I urged him to decide at once. On his knees in his cabin, he received the Lord Jesus. He has three times given his testimony. His whole life has changed. Most of the day is taken up with reading the Bible. Praise the Lord! It is lovely. Not only have these been brought to the Lord but also several of the stewards. You can imagine what a change that means among the ship's company.

C. T. Studd

There were many conversations about the Lord Jesus on board the ship, but many off it too. As the vessel pulled into various ports – at Brindisi, Suez, Alexandria, Colombo, Penang, Singapore and Hong Kong – the Cambridge Seven disembarked to meet people and tell them the good news about Jesus Christ. Not surprisingly they left a trail of blessings as they docked in one port after another. Many people believed and were added to the number of those being saved around the world.

On the 1st of April, 1885, the young men disembarked at Shanghai. The expectation of the C.I.M. was for their missionaries to submerge themselves in local language, dress, and culture.

'Shave my head?!' blurted Monty Beauchamp as the barber drew closer with a razor in his hand. 'Me first?'

'You knew it was going to happen,' said C.T.

'Yes. But I thought you'd go first,' said Monty, looking at him. Monty plonked himself on to a hard wooden stool and braced himself for the impending transformation.

'Afraid you'll get cold?' laughed Stanley.

'He'll not shave it all off,' C.T. assured him.

'He'll leave you a pigtail!' snorted William.

Monty's face grew redder. 'Then he can take the moustache too,' he conceded.

'You don't have to lose the 'stache, Monty,' said Dixon. Monty didn't hear him.

'Hey, chaps, look at these!' said Arthur, holding up some dark-coloured, traditional Chinese clothes that

From Cricket to Christ

he found in a basket at the other end of the room. 'Are these for us?'

'It's a far cry from English attire,' chortled his brother Cecil.

'I think we will look ridiculous dressed in those,' C.T. guffawed.

Later that morning, the process of transformation was complete and it was time for a photograph to mark the occasion. C.T., Monty, and Stanley, being the tallest, stood behind four chairs on which the other men sat. They hid their awkwardness well as the photo was being taken.

Now that the Seven were in China, they prepared to part company. After all, they were in that vast country to bring the gospel of Jesus to as many people as possible.

On 4th April C.T. and the Polhill-Turner brothers boarded a boat and began their journey to Hanchung by way of the Yangste and Han Rivers. From Hanchung they planned to walk northward to meet Hudson Taylor at Pingyang-Fu. They anticipated it would be a long and arduous journey.

C.T. needed a good pair of shoes for the trek. As his feet were so much bigger than that of an average Chinese man, he knew finding shoes to fit was going to be a hard job. It hadn't been a problem on the boats; he'd gotten away with wearing his straw sandals. However, if he was going to walk the pathways of inland China, he was going to have to get some appropriate footwear.

C.T. Studd

The first shoemaker simply declared that he couldn't do it, and ran away from the sheer size of the task. Thankfully C.T. found another shoemaker who was up for the challenge.

'I have made many, many shoes for many, many years,' said the shoemaker as he knelt before C.T. to fit his new shoes. 'But I have never made anything like these before,' he added dryly. 'Stand and walk,' he commanded C.T.

C.T. stood and walked a few paces this way and that. His new shoes fitted but they were uncomfortable. 'They'll do rightly,' said C.T. to an amused shoemaker who had never seen anything quite so odd as this tall, Chinese-looking Englishman with huge feet standing before him.

Now that C.T got his shoes, he and the other missionaries continued the slow journey to Hanchung. They spent their time trying to learn the Chinese language from a teacher on board who had no knowledge of English whatsoever. The young men couldn't wait to be fluent, such was their desire to tell the Chinese of the good news of Jesus in the local language.

As promised, C.T. wrote many letters home to his mother and siblings during the trip. His two youngest brothers, Reggie and Bertie, were at Eton. C.T. felt the need to counsel them about sport and other recreational activities at school. He was especially qualified to offer them advice about these things.

From Cricket to Christ

'I do not say, Don't play games or cricket and so forth. By all means play and enjoy them, giving thanks to Jesus for them. Only take care that games do not become an idol to you, as they did to me. What good will it do anybody in the next world to have been even the best player that has ever been? And then think of the difference between that and winning souls for Jesus. Oh, if you have never tasted the joy of leading one soul to Jesus, go and ask our Father to enable you to do so, and then you will know what true joy is! The time is so short, such little time to rescue souls from hell, for there will be no rescue work in heaven. I have written earnestly because I know the joy there is in Jesus and because I well know the innumerable temptations you are exposed to in a Public School life.'[1]

Disembarking at Hanchung, the missionaries and their assistants headed north for the rendezvous with Hudson Taylor at Pingyang-Fu. The plan was to walk thirty miles a day or nearly fifty kilometres. Even at that pace, it was going to take several weeks to complete the journey. Along the way, the men stopped for food in villages. At night they usually slept on the communal floors of local inns. It was tough going, especially for C.T.'s feet in those uncomfortable shoes. Most of the time he was in unbearable pain.

'Hold on a minute,' yelped C.T. from the back of the group. 'I have to take these shoes off.' He sat on

---

1. *C.T. Studd, Cricketer and Pioneer*, by Norman P. Grubb (The Lutterworth Press, Cambridge, 1933) page 53.

C.T. Studd

the ground. Arthur and Cecil doubled back to C.T.'s position to check on him. They watched him slowly take his shoes off to reveal blistering sore feet, red raw in places.

'Ouch, that looks really painful,' remarked Cecil.

'Can you get my sandals out of my bag for me, please?' C.T. asked Arthur.

'Yes, of course,' replied Arthur as he began to rummage around in the bag to locate the sandals. 'Got them. Here you go,' he said, and handed them to his wounded friend.

'Can you keep going, or do you need to rest?' asked Cecil.

'No, let's keep going, Cecil. The good Lord will give me the strength to carry on.' C.T. forced a smile as he got back to his feet. His mental fortitude was strong, having been built by years of playing cricket. By God's help and with sheer grit and determination, C.T. was confident he would reach Pingyang-Fu with his companions. The group kept up their desired pace that day, and C.T. praised God for the strength to do it, although each step in the straw sandals proved agonising for him.

He started out in the sandals the following day, but after twelve miles (about nineteen kilometres) he had to take them off and continue on barefoot. Subsequent miles of agony ensued. The group thought that a horse for the lame missionary would help, but they were unable to find one.

From Cricket to Christ

There seemed to be little sympathy for C.T.'s plight from the local assistants, who wanted to push on quickly by increasing the distance of their daily hike. Each day, C.T. fell further behind the others, until he ended up walking mostly on his own. But he spent the time praying and giving thanks to God for his presence with him and for God's strength to endure the suffering he was experiencing. He asked one of the group to pray with him and anoint his feet with oil in the name of the Lord, according to the instruction he read in the letter of James[2]. Over the days that followed, C.T. noticed his feet getting better, and the swelling continued going down, until the pain was finally gone.

When they arrived in Pingyang-Fu, Hudson Taylor was there to greet them. The next few days saw C.T. and the Polhill-Turners relaying to Hudson the hilarious transformation story in Shanghai, as well as the challenge of the journey from Hanchung to Pingyang-Fu.

Then Hudson asked them, 'How's the language study coming along?'

'Not so well,' disclosed Arthur.

'It's a very difficult language,' admitted Cecil.

'We have been in constant prayer and fasting about it, Hudson. We believe that the Lord will miraculously give us mastery of the language,' C.T. confessed.

'Without studying for it?' asked Hudson incredulously.

---

2. James 5:14-15.

C. T. Studd

'Will the Lord not give us all things if we ask him in faith?' came Arthur's rhetorical reply.

'After all, we believe in miracles, Hudson,' added Cecil.

Hudson was quiet and thoughtful as the young missionaries explained their reasons for abandoning language study. Then he said, 'If I could put Chinese into your heads with the wave of my hand, I would still not do it.'

The young missionaries could feel a gentle reprimand coming. Hudson explained the importance of learning the language from their teacher and friends. Listening and learning from their teacher would not only help them grasp the language, but also encourage them to grow in wisdom and understanding of the culture in which they served.

C.T. admitted that they had perhaps made a mistake and promised to resume language study. His understanding of Chinese was helped along by his next assignment: Hudson asked C.T. to go to a C.I.M mission station at Chin-Wu to keep it open. There were no C.I.M missionaries there so he would be on his own. He jumped at the chance to submerge himself completely among the Chinese people, and his time at Chin-Wu gave him just what he needed – a greater confidence in the Chinese language and a deeper understanding of Chinese culture. Without doubt, he was settling in well and enjoying his ministry there. Every day he sought opportunities to speak to his neighbours about Jesus.

From Cricket to Christ

It was a peaceful time for C.T. in Chin-Wu, considering foreigners, or 'foreign devils' as they were called by the locals, were not always welcome throughout China. For now, he thanked God for the honeymoon period. He knew persecution and suffering would eventually come his way, as it does to all who trust in Christ.

A Great Giveaway

'It has come to my attention that riots have broken out in the Province of Szechwan,' said Hudson Taylor to his assembled C.I.M missionaries in Hanchung. In the midst of them sat C.T. who had returned from Chin-Wu earlier that summer. It was the Autumn of 1886, and C.T. wondered where the Lord would send him next.

'Anyone hurt?' enquired one of the older missionaries.

'People have been hurt, properties have been destroyed, and many foreigners have fled the district of Chungking,' Hudson replied. 'It's a challenging situation there and it has left the area without any Christian witnesses.' He paused briefly and inhaled. 'Who wants to go into Szechwan Province?'

Everyone volunteered. Hudson was encouraged by his team's heroism. He chose C.T. to go to Chungking, accompanied by another missionary known as Mr Phelps.

The two volunteers stopped in the city of Pauling on their south-easterly journey from Hanchung to Chungking. They sensed a heightened spirit of suspicion and unease from people as they walked along the streets of the city. It was clear to the missionaries that news

From Cricket to Christ

of the riots at Chungking had reached the ears of the people of Pauling.

'I don't like the way some people are looking at us,' Phelps said quietly, barely moving his lips.

'Just ignore them and keep walking. Let's see if we can find somewhere to stay for the night.'

One by one the fearful innkeepers turned the missionaries away. They did not want to be accused of sheltering 'foreign devils' by any disapproving relatives or neighbours.

That night the men found a windowless room to lay their heads. It was next to a pigsty. The partition wall between the room and the pigsty was nothing more than a few thin pieces of board; it wasn't thick enough to keep out the foul smell coming from the pigs. Sleep did not totally elude them that night, but it wasn't the best night's kip they'd had since being in China.

The next day, C.T. and Phelps pushed on through the city of Pauling. When the evening came, they found a small inn that was willing to harbour them for the night. It even had a window! But it surpassed the previous place in foul odours.

'Whew, that smell is even worse than last night,' whispered Phelps in C.T.'s ear.

'Look on the positive side, Phelps. It has a window.'

'It's not open. Doesn't it open? It should really be open, to let that foul odour escape.'

C.T. gently slapped him on the back. 'It'll be fine.'

C.T. Studd

But it wasn't fine. Not only did the bad smell make breathing uncomfortable, C.T. woke in the middle of the night to find himself being attacked by bugs that had invaded the room under the cover of darkness. There were hundreds of them. C.T. defended himself valiantly for an hour or so against the mini onslaught, then went back to sleep. He was battle-weary but strangely good humoured.

In the morning, after reading the Word of God and praying, the men set off for their final destination – Chungking. Upon approaching, they saw what appeared to be guards posted at the gates into the city. But the young missionaries were able to pass by them without any interference. They headed for the British Consulate and were greeted by an astonished Consul called Mr Bourne.

'However did you get here?' he gasped in astonishment, as if he were looking at a couple of ghosts. 'There are guards on every gate in the city to prevent any "foreign devils" from coming in.'

'Yes, we saw them,' Phelps confirmed.

'God brought us in to the city, sir. And we are here on God's business: the saving of lost souls through our Lord Jesus Christ,' C.T. said.

'No, you cannot stay here, gentlemen,' asserted Mr Bourne. 'I can give you a passport up or down the river, but no foreigners are allowed here, except myself.'

C.T. insisted they were there to do the Lord's work and, given the dire circumstances that led to their

From Cricket to Christ

arrival, they would not be deviated from the mission. Mr Bourne listened carefully as the argument for staying in Chungking was graciously but firmly made by the young men. It was clear to him they would not leave.

Phelps asked him if there was any suitable accommodation in the area. Mr Bourne pointed to a run-down building and said, 'You can stay in that hovel over there, but there is only room for one of you.'

The young men began to discuss who would stay in Chungking. Both of them were keen to do it. Mr Bourne interrupted their deliberations with an invitation to dinner. They gladly accepted and headed off to dine with the Consul.

Halfway through dinner, Mr Bourne put a question to C.T.

'Studd, will you stay with me?'

And that was it. The matter of who was to remain in Chungking was resolved.

'Yes. I would be delighted to, Mr Bourne. Thank you,' replied C.T.

Phelps was dignified in defeat, although it wasn't a contest. He just wanted to serve the Lord, same as his old pal Studd. Phelps returned to Hanchung, leaving C.T. to embark on a most challenging venture for the Lord in a distant part of Southwest China.

While he was in Chungking, C.T. turned twenty-five years of age. It was a significant birthday for him, because it was the age that his father designated for him to receive his inheritance. C.T. received a sizeable sum of money from his late father's estate, and he had already thought and prayed earnestly about what he would do with it.

He had searched the Scriptures diligently and was particularly struck by a passage in Luke 18, the account of the 'Rich Ruler'. The ruler was an attractive guy. He had a place of power and he had earned it. He was the epitome of success, and he was even polite. He approached Jesus and told him that he had done a lot of good things in his life and had amassed many good things. Now it was time to add eternal life to his portfolio. 'What must I do to enter eternal life?' he asked Jesus. But eternal life is not something that you can earn. Humanity is lost; eternal life is a free gift from God.[1]

Although the ruler was successful, Jesus saw that he was lost and in the grip of a monstrous idol which threatened to take eternal life away from him. Jesus pointed him to the Commandments. The rich ruler waved his hand and said, 'Yes, I have kept them all.' But Jesus knew that the ruler had not kept the first command of God – 'You shall have no other gods before me.'

So Jesus touched the idol that had gripped the ruler's heart and said to him, 'One thing you still lack. Sell all that you have and distribute to the poor and you will have treasure in heaven; and come, follow me.'

Jesus said these words, not because poverty was more spiritual than being wealthy nor because a grand

---

1. Romans 6:23.

From Cricket to Christ

gesture was somehow going to save the rich ruler, but because it was a simple matter of what was most precious to the man. Jesus challenged the ruler to let go of the idol of wealth that was gripping his heart and was killing him spiritually, and to see that true treasure is found only in Jesus.

C.T. had been surrounded by people who thought that riches brought happiness, and that great wealth brought great joy. But he knew that without Jesus, there is no joy. And C.T. knew how to spell 'J-O-Y' – Jesus, Others, Yourself, in that order. He would not let his wealth stand between him and his precious Lord Jesus. He was going to give his fortune away to gospel endeavours around the world – to help people hear the gospel of Jesus and receive the gift of eternal life.

The amount of £29,000[2] was at his disposal. C.T. went to Mr Bourne and had him draw up official papers, enabling the young missionary to distribute the funds to whomever he had prayerfully chosen.

In January 1887, C.T. sat down at his table and wrote four huge cheques for £5,000 each, and five smaller cheques for £1,000. He kept back the remainder for the time being, until he could work out what to do with it.

The first cheque was sent to D.L. Moody in the hope that he could set up a gospel ministry in India, where C.T.'s late father had made his vast fortune before returning to England. Unfortunately Mr Moody

---

2. In 2024, C.T.'s inheritance would be worth just under £5 million.

C.T. Studd

was unable to fulfil this desire, and instead used the money to set up a Bible college in Chicago, U.S.A. It was called the 'Chicago Evangelization Society' and was later renamed the 'Moody Bible Institute'.

The second cheque went to George Müller in Bristol, England. Mr Müller had organised the opening of a number of orphanages and had cared for many children. He prayed and trusted God alone for the provision of their daily needs, a principle that also inspired C.T. in his ministry for the Lord. Mr Müller was encouraged to divide the money: £4,000 for Mr Müller's missionary work in England, and £1,000 for the care of the orphans.

The third cheque arrived with Mr George Holland, whose ministry among the poor of London was close to C.T.'s heart.

The fourth cheque was for Commissioner Booth Tucker and the work of the Salvation Army in India. The money was used to train and send out new workers among the poor there.

The five smaller amounts of £1,000 were sent to worthy gospel ministries in London and Dublin, including the Salvation Army and Dr Barnardo for his children's homes.

Mr Bourne was amazed by C.T.'s generosity. He had tried to encourage the young missionary to think carefully before giving it all away. He quietly hoped C.T. would see sense and keep most of the money for his own well-being. But C.T. did not share such a

From Cricket to Christ

worldly view of things. If his money could be used to help people hear the gospel of Jesus Christ and enter into the eternal dwellings of God, then there was no greater place to put his money than the Bank of Heaven.

Having already written to thank C.T. for the generous gift, Commissioner Booth Tucker put pen to paper once more, informing the young benefactor of the way the money was going to be used.

'My very dear Brother,
I have been waiting to write to you until I could give you some more definite news as to the special advances we hope to make by means of the help you have sent us. You will be glad to hear that the first result is a positive promise from General William Booth to send us fifty first-class officers as soon as possible. This is grand.... Our war is full of intense interest. We really never know what a day may bring forth. One hour we are fingering our food into our mouths, (do you use chopsticks in China?), the next we are opening a letter from an anonymous friend with a donation of £5000!... You would, I am sure, delight in roughing it with us, or perhaps after your Chinese experiences it would appear smooth enough to you. I feel sure that you will say with our dear Indian Officers – 'We would rather have the hardest station out here than the easiest in London.' Our party have no salaries, get no money, and having food and clothing, they learn to be content with that. No grumbling or arguing can be heard in our camp. Both lads and lassies go barefoot (for preference).

C.T. Studd

For meals they have rice water in the morning, rice and vegetable curries (no meat) at midday and the same in the evening. The use of tea and coffee is quite given up as being too European! The floor of the quarters being well raised and dug, we have abolished beds. There are no chairs and tables in the camp. I am myself sitting squatted on a mat, with my papers around me on the floor. Nevertheless, we are very comfortable and as happy as possible. Most beautiful of all has been the spirit of unity, love, devotion and sacrifice which has animated them all from the first. . . . The Lord of the Harvest abundantly bless you, and enable you to see and fall in line with his notions for a present-day salvation sweep. Oh, that we may see eye to eye with the Lord in his plans for saving men!'

Soon after, C.T. left Chungking and headed to Shanghai on the coast of the East China Sea. He was aware that his brother, George, was touring some warmer climates for the sake of his health, and he was going to meet him in that city.

Little did C.T. know that he would meet someone else in Shanghai – someone who would completely change his life.

Meeting Priscilla

The C.I.M. guest house was under the care of Miss Black, a congenial soul who made everyone feel welcome. She was not the only person living in the home when C.T. arrived in the Spring of 1887.

A Scotsman, Mr John Stevenson, was also staying in the guest house. He had been part of the C.I.M. family since 1864 and had started working in China the following year, in 1865. Mr Stevenson was spending some time in the guest house before moving on to some of the farther outposts to visit the missionaries serving God in the country. This was part of his role as Deputy Director of C.I.M. Mr Stevenson was expected to visit places to which Mr Hudson Taylor could not personally go and to lead the Mission, especially if Mr Taylor was not in the country. Immediately after Mr Stevenson agreed to Mr Taylor's decision to make him Deputy Director, he was sent to distant outposts to call upon, learn from, and encourage the missionaries. In the meantime, Mr Stevenson's wife, Anne, and his children, were back in his homeland of Scotland.

Like most people around the world who serve for Jesus Christ on the mission field, Mr Stevenson had his fair share of disease and sickness. He had been afflicted

From Cricket to Christ

with malaria[1], typhoid fever[2] and smallpox.[3.] Having recovered from smallpox, Mr Stevenson noticed that the disease left pockmarks in his skin. According to his Chinese neighbours it was a sign of death-defying 'good luck'.

The other guest was a young woman called Miss Priscilla Livingstone Stewart, from the northern part of Ireland. She was descended from the entrepreneurial Stewart family who owned and operated the Stewarts' Linen Mills of Lisburn in County Antrim. Priscilla grew up in a traditional Church of Ireland, but after her conversion to Christ as a young woman she felt more at home in the church services of the Salvation Army.

It was during evening tea on the first night of C.T.'s stay that Mr Stevenson asked him about his plans whilst in Shanghai. The ladies listened on intently.

C.T. said, 'My brother George will be arriving in the city any day. I hope to spend some time with him before he moves on in his journey to find warmer places.'

Mr Stevenson look quizzically at C.T. who continued, 'Oh, due to his health. The doctors have

---

1. Malaria is a serious infection that is transmitted by mosquitoes. It can cause death if it is not diagnosed or treated quickly.

2. Typhoid fever is a bacterial infection that can affect the organs in the body. If it is not treated promptly it can cause organ complications and can also be fatal.

3. Declared eradicated by the World Health Organisation in 1980, smallpox was a viral infection that produced blisters on the skin. These blisters would scab over, fall off, and leave scars on the victim, commonly referred to as pockmarks.

said that warmer weather will suit him better than the British climate.'

Mr Stevenson nodded understandingly. The weather in the British Isles was known for being generally wet and grey, and not especially good for anyone who suffered with breathing or lung complaints, as George did.

'And have you given any prayerful thought to what you'll do for the Lord while you're here?' asked Mr Stevenson.

'Well, the dialect here is different to where I've been serving. I guess I will struggle to tell them the good news about Jesus in their own language. So, I was thinking of doing some ministry amongst the sailors.'

'There are some British naval ships in the port at the moment. The "Soldiers' Rest" will be bustling,' Mr Stevenson remarked.

'What a wonderful opportunity for the gospel!' Miss Black exclaimed.

'Yes it is. And you are all welcome to join me,' said C.T. as he looked at Priscilla.

It was customary to begin each day in prayer at the guest house. C.T. pulled Mr Stevenson aside for a quiet word.

'I received a most remarkable letter from General William Booth of the Salvation Army. May I share it with the others at the prayer meeting please? I think they will find it most encouraging.'

From Cricket to Christ

Mr Stevenson agreed. As the guests sat down together for prayer, C.T. opened the letter and began to read about the challenges and triumphs of serving Christ in India and reaching the lost with the good news of Christ.

C.T. noticed how each listener was impacted by the letter, and by Priscilla in particular. She was clearly moved by it, so much so that she began to attend the nightly meetings at the Soldiers' Rest, and she became more vocal in her witness for the Lord.

When he first met her, C.T. was unsure of her suitability for missionary work in the centre of China. Mr Stevenson had asked him for his opinion about her. C.T. had noticed how, due to a heart condition that impeded her physical fitness, she often laboured up the stairs of the guesthouse. Inland China was a hard place. Perhaps too hard for Priscilla. C.T. wondered if maybe it was a mistake for Priscilla to be in Shanghai, or even China at all. But now she seemed invigorated, the fire in her heart burning all the more brightly for the Lord. At the meetings in the Soldiers' Rest, the men hung on her every word, and her words pointed to Jesus Christ and salvation in him alone.

C.T. was quietly impressed with her zeal and love for Jesus. He began to look at Priscilla in a new light, not as a sickly and misplaced person, but as a fellow warrior for Christ in the battle to win souls for the glory of God. Many were converted at those meetings in the Soldiers' Rest and went back to their ships as

C.T. Studd

changed men, born of God and full of his Spirit. Life on board their vessels was different; as these new Christian sailors sought the betterment of their shipmates, rather than encouraging them in drunkenness and wayward living as they did before.

George finally turned up in Shanghai and roomed with his brother at the C.I.M. guesthouse. Although George was a converted man, C.T. knew that his brother had grown somewhat cold in his love for the Lord Jesus over the years. C.T. thought it best not to speak to George about spiritual things, at least not for the time being. He prayed for wisdom, knowing that God's timing in these matters, indeed in all things, was perfect.

The day after he arrived, George booked a ticket to sail to Japan. He had planned on staying with C.T. just long enough to catch up with him without outstaying his welcome. He enjoyed his time there, playing cricket in a local club and showing people how to play it exceptionally well. C.T. cheered him from the sidelines. Of course, the Studds' reputation for cricket had preceded them, and people again questioned the sanity of the magnificent all-round cricketer C.T. Studd giving up absolutely everything to move out to China as a missionary. Surprisingly, it was George who stood up in a public meeting that week and told all those Shanghai doubters that C.T. was most certainly in his right mind doing what he did for Jesus Christ!

From Cricket to Christ

In the end, George never did set foot on the ship sailing for Japan. 'I would like to go with you, dear brother,' said George as they took a stroll down the main market street near the guesthouse.

'But I'm heading back inland, George. Are you sure? I mean, I would love to have you with me, of course I would.'

'Yes, I'm sure. Where are you going, do you know?'

'Likely north to Taiyuan-Fu. It's the chief town in the Province of Shanxi.'

'Sounds splendid,' smiled George. 'When do we leave?'

'Soon enough, George. Soon enough.'

They walked a bit further through the bustling market, with George being distracted by one seller after another, each person trying to entice his money into their pockets. The brothers' conversation waned for a moment, allowing C.T.'s mind to wander to Priscilla, the blue-eyed, red-haired lass from Lisburn. C.T. had grown extremely fond of her over the short time they had been together in Shanghai. He was not looking forward to their parting. He had an inkling that she felt the same way, but neither had said anything about their attraction to each other. He would bring it to the Lord in prayer.

Priscilla was feeling much better. It was almost time for her to move on from Shanghai. Eventually she received word of her new mission posting to Ta-Ku-T'ang, a small fishing town situated at the extreme north of the Po-Yang Lake in the Kiang-si Province of

62

C. T. Studd

central China. She would be accompanied by three other female missionaries, so at least she would not be alone in her work there. C.T felt comforted by that, although he knew that a Christian was never alone because Christ, in Matthew's Gospel,[4] promised to always be with his people.

When Priscilla left Shanghai, C.T. fasted and prayed to God for eight days before concluding that he should ask her to marry him. In July 1887, from his mission post in Taiyuan-Fu, C.T. put pen to paper. Devoid of romance, he wrote an honest letter of the life they would have together.

> It will be no easy life, no life of ease which I could offer you, but one of toil and hardship; in fact, if I did not know you to be a woman of God, I would not dream of asking you. It is to be a fellow soldier in His Army. It is to live a life of faith in God, a fighting life, remembering that here we have no abiding city, no certain dwelling-place but only a home eternal in the Father's House above. Such would be the life: may the Lord alone guide you.

Priscilla's refusal surprised him. She did not feel that God wanted them to be together as husband and wife. Undeterred, C.T. wrote again, chastising Priscilla for her lack of faith:

> You have neither the mind of God, nor the will of God in the matter, but I have. And I intend to marry

---

4. Matthew 28:20.

From Cricket to Christ

you whether you will or not, so you'd better make
up your mind and accept the situation!

The communications by letter went back and forth until
Priscilla finally agreed to his proposal in October. An
elated C.T. could not contain the happiness he felt by
her acceptance:

I must write and tell darling mother this mail, and
others too, for I cannot keep it secret; only I do
laugh when I think of how little I know of or about
you, my own darling, not even your age or anything;
only it is more than enough for me that you are a
true child and lover of the Lord Jesus, that He has
knit my heart to yours and yours to mine to work
together for Him with all our hearts and souls and
minds until He come.

C.T. wrote to his darling mother back in England,
although his letter had limited details concerning his
future wife.

I suppose you want to know about her. 'Well, to tell
you the truth, I can't tell you much except about her
spiritual life and her life before the world; I don't
even know her age, but guess she is some years my
junior, don't know though. She ain't very big, and
as regards her face, well, she has the beauty of the
Lord her God upon her, which is worth more than
all the beauty of the whole world. She writes a very
good letter, all about Jesus, and naturally a big hand
except when she has a lot to say; she can run up and

C.T. Studd

downstairs a tremendous pace; she can also play the harmonium or organ and sing a bit, but her voice wasn't wonderful in Shanghai. She's very fond of the Salvation Army hymns (so am I), and of the Salvation Army too (so am I), and she doesn't fear the face of man or woman a little bit, I do believe; but just fires away at everybody she meets about their souls. I haven't got a photo of her at all, so I cannot give you even a guess at what she is like; probably Georgie is a better hand at such descriptions and will be able to satisfy your curiosity. Oh! I know one thing more; her name is Priscilla Livingstone Stewart, and she calls herself 'Scilla. Why not 'Pris'? I don't understand, but then she's Irish!'[5]

The young missionary couple had an unofficial wedding at Priscilla's mission station officiated by a Chinese evangelist. She wore a long white sash with the words 'United to fight for Jesus' on it. They knelt and promised one another that they would never hinder each other from serving the Lord.

C.T. and Priscilla travelled to Tientsin on the shore of the Bohai Sea in northern China, to be married officially by the British Consul in residence there. They were officially Mr and Mrs Studd on the 7th of April, 1888.

Together at last, Lungang-Fu was the next mission assignment for the newly weds. They discovered from the outset that it was a dangerous place for foreigners, especially those who proclaimed the gospel of Christ.

5. *C.T. Studd, Cricketer and Pioneer,* by Norman P. Grubb (The Lutterworth Press, Cambridge, 1933) page 78.

No Foreign Devils Here!

The priority for the newly weds was a place to live. Vacant accommodation was scarce in Lungan-Fu, especially for 'foreign devils' like them. A local man was willing to condescend to speak with them and told the couple there was only one house available in the city. It was empty for good reason. Everyone believed it was haunted, so no Chinese person would ever live there. Undeterred, C.T and Priscilla marched in the direction that the man told them to look, in search of their new home. C.T. was confident that the Lord would expel any devils when they arrived in his name.

The house was in bad repair having been left abandoned for a long time. The walls were whitewashed. The floor was made of brick, poorly laid and uneven. They made a mental note to be careful not to stub their toes on raised bricks as they walked across it. The fireplace was in the middle of the room and in the far corner was the bed. It was made out of brick too. Little scorpions darted in and out of the crevasses of the bed's poor construction and scurried across the floor in search of other hiding places in the room.

'What do you think, Scilla?'

'It'll do rightly, Charlie.'

From Cricket to Christ

Outside in the courtyard, there was an area large enough for C.T. to eventually erect a small chapel for meetings.

Another missionary had accompanied them to Lungan-Fu. Miss Mary Burroughs was a friend and fellow worker of Priscilla's, and she was looking forward to the challenge of ministry in a city where there were no other European faces, and no knowledge of Christ Jesus. Thankfully the house had enough space for all of them, which was a real blessing especially when Miss Edith Bewes, another C.I.M. worker, joined the missionary group a short while later to assist in the work.

The locals were not accustomed to foreigners, and treated them with the utmost suspicion. The bottom line was that the Chinese simply did not like them. Whenever they left the house, the missionaries were constantly bombarded with vile and offensive utterances from their neighbours.

Not surprisingly, everything that was wrong with the world was blamed on the Christians – a common occurrence experienced by servants of the Lord Jesus down through the centuries. An ignorant, excitable, credulous population hated what they did not understand. A slump in trade at the marketplace or a natural calamity, such as an earthquake, flood, or drought would send the people clamouring for vengeance against the Christians.

Early on in the missionaries' time at Lungan-Fu, a drought gripped the area. C.T. was alarmed to learn

C.T. Studd

of a most devious plot to hurt them because they were being blamed by the neighbours for the lack of rain.

On a trip to the market, he saw placards that had been hoisted high for everyone to see. A set of instructions were written on them, telling the public to close the doors of their courtyards in a few days. Outside they were to burn incense as a fragrant offering to the rain god – most likely 'Yu Shi,' the Chinese god of rain – whose statue would be processed through the streets of the city and who would hopefully reverse the drought and bring rain to the region. A group of men were already on their way to a nearby city to collect the stone figure and bring it to Lungan-Fu.

The people of Lungan-Fu knew well that the Christian missionaries would not burn incense to a Chinese god. This gave them the perfect excuse to attack the 'foreign devils' and drive them from their midst.

C.T. hurried back to tell Priscilla and Mary about the plan. Priscilla wasn't feeling too well, and C.T. knew he would have to help her evacuate the house when the time came for it.

'They know we won't do it,' Priscilla said weakly.

'Of course they do,' C.T. confirmed.

'There'll be a riot on our doorstep, no doubt about that,' Mary chipped in, when she heard the news.

'We'll have to be ready for it,' C.T. replied. 'The first thing we do, Mary, is pray.' She nodded in agreement.

They gathered around Priscilla who was lying on the bed, and brought the whole terrible situation before

69

From Cricket to Christ

the Lord in prayer. They prayed long into the night, then fell asleep.

The next day, sweet smelling incense filled the air. The noise of a raucous crowd grew closer as the missionaries braced themselves for what was going to be an extremely tense situation. They were conscious that their reactions to their neighbours at this juncture would be scrutinised for a long time to come. They wanted to be like Jesus, and they asked him to help them.

The mob gathered outside the mission station, intent on causing harm to their foreign neighbours. They roared and screamed as they began to pull down the walls of the chapel. C.T. gathered Priscilla up into his arms and brought her out into the courtyard.

'Stay here,' he said to her as he gently laid her on the ground. 'I'm going to the mandarins to get help.'

The mandarins were local officials whose duties involved governing local towns and cities. It was a long shot to get help from the mandarins, as they also did not want the Christian missionaries in their area. But C.T. knew it was the right thing to do. He was going to the local officials to ask them to bring wisdom, law, and order to a local disturbance.

Incredibly, when he got to the mandarins' hall, he discovered they were not in the city, presumably in an attempt not to have to deal with the consequences of the riot. He quickly turned tail and headed back to the mission station as fast as he could.

C. T. Studd

Meanwhile the disturbance at the mission station was getting worse. The plan to terrorise the missionaries into leaving China forever was in full flow. The mob screamed death threats while they pelted the mission station with missiles made of brick and glass. The chapel was now alight. Naturally the missionaries were petrified by the ferocity of their neighbour's words and actions. They prayed fervently that the Lord would deliver them from the evil that encompassed them.

Suddenly a shrill voice could be heard through the din. 'What are you doing?!'

A well-respected teacher was bravely challenging the viciousness of the crowd. Some of the rioters stopped and looked at him. As the hubbub began to subside, he shouted again, 'What are you doing?!'

All eyes were now trained on him, and all ears were straining to hear him, so he continued. 'While you are wasting the time, the day is passing, and if you do not take the god on quickly, he will not feel the sun on his own head. Take him on, and then come back this way.'

Like meek children, they dropped their projectiles and attended to their god made of stone. They picked it up and processed away from the mission station in an attempt to catch the sun's rays on its head and end the drought.

The next few days saw the missionaries dealing with the destruction done to their home. C.T. reminded them it was only property. Things can be fixed. They

From Cricket to Christ

were all thankful to God that they were physically unharmed despite the mob's intentions.

Strengthened by the Lord, the missionaries were all the more resolved to remain with the people of Lungan-Fu. 'These people are lost, and Jesus has come to seek and to save the lost,' C.T. reminded them.

The Christlike way in which the small team from C.I.M. dealt with the violence against them was noted by the community. Some even dared speak with them about the Christian religion.

Meetings were regularly held at the mission station and the locals were invited to hear the gospel. One night C.T. preached a sermon on the Bible text, 'He is able to save to the uttermost those who draw near to God through Jesus.'[1] A surly looking man sat at the back of the room. He appeared unconvinced of what C.T. was saying about Jesus' ability to save even the most wicked offenders.

As the meeting came to an end, the room began to empty, allowing the man to approach the preacher, determined to make the point that he was unredeemable. Standing before C.T., he looked him straight in the eye and unabashedly confessed, 'I am a murderer. I am an adulterer. I have broken all the laws of God and man again and again. I am also a confirmed opium smoker. Jesus cannot save me!'

'Do you want to be saved?' C.T. asked him directly. The man was taken aback by the question and gave no

1. Hebrews 7:25.

C.T. Studd

immediate response. C.T. explained the gospel of Jesus as clearly as he could and called on the man to repent of his sins and believe in the Lord Jesus Christ. That evening, the man was wonderfully converted and left the building rejoicing in his salvation.

Feeling compelled by Christ to return to his hometown, the man vowed to seek forgiveness from those he had wronged and pledged to tell as many as he could about the saving love of Jesus.

Vast crowds gathered to hear this new evangelist proclaim the good news about Jesus and his love for them, much to the consternation of the local mandarin. The mandarin ordered the preacher to be arrested and sentenced him to receive 2,000 lashes using bamboo canes. His back was blistered and red, and the pain was excruciating. The man fell unconscious during the punishment, presumed dead. But he was alive, just barely.

Friends took him to a hospital where he was nursed back to health by those who loved and followed Jesus. Over time the man was able to sit up in bed. He announced to his friends that he had to go back to home and preach the gospel once again to his neighbours. The missionaries of Lungan-Fu heard about his desire and tried, in vain, to dissuade him.

Escaping from hospital, he returned to his place of torture, and preached the gospel with boldness to those who had rejected him before. He was arrested once again and brought before the mandarin. This time the mandarin had the evangelist thrown in prison.

From Cricket to Christ

Through the holes in the walls and cracks in the prison doors the man preached to his fellow prisoners. A small window of his dank prison cell was the perfect opening for the man to preach the gospel to people passing by outside. Crowds began to gather around the window to hear his message about Jesus. The preacher was causing quite a stir in the town. Clearly he would not be silenced.

What should be done with such a stubborn man? the mandarin thought. *Should he be put to death? Or should he be released and told to go away?* God answered the prayers of his people for the man, and he was released from his incarceration, to continue the mission of proclaiming Christ to all who would hear. The man testified personally that Christ was indeed able to save to the uttermost.

In his confession to C.T. the converted man admitted to being an opium smoker. Opium was a drug manufactured from the unripe seeds of the opium poppy. From its introduction into the country from Turkey in the late sixth or early seventh century, opium was initially used for pain relief. However, opium smoking had become a serious problem due to its addictive properties which often led to overdose and death.

C.T. and his fellow workers opened an opium refuge in Lungan-Fu. They wanted to help men and women come off the drug, get clean, and turn their lives around. Of course, they would tell their patients the gospel of Jesus when opportunities arose. But as good

C.T. Studd

and obedient servants of Christ, C.T. and the others looked after everyone in the same way. Whether the addict turned to Christ in repentance and faith or not, each person would receive the same loving kindness and care from the missionaries.

A lot of time was spent helping the men and women of the district who were addicted to opium. The days were long. The work was hard and ceaseless. By 1894, they were able to look after fifty residents at a time. Most were men; some were women. There were even a few children who passed through the door of the refuge asking for help.

During their ministry in Lungan-Fu, C.T. and Priscilla reckoned at least eight hundred people received treatment at their refuge. Some left the refuge cured of their addictions; some left the refuge as Christians. The vilification that the Studds received from their neighbours during the early days in Lungan-Fu became a distant memory. They praised the Lord that they did not leave the area after the drought riot, because now they were witnessing some of their Chinese neighbours become brothers and sisters in Christ.

God was blessing their faithful ministry in Lungan-Fu, and God blessed them as a family too. Four beautiful daughters were born in that foreign land. Grace was the first, in 1889. It was a difficult pregnancy, and Priscilla became ill after the birth. Unfortunately Mary Burroughs was also incapacitated with sickness and was therefore out of action at this time.

From Cricket to Christ

C.T. did the best he could to care for Priscilla, but he was thankful for the relief provided by Miss Jessie Kerr, a skilled nurse who arrived a few days after Grace was born. After spending a short period of time in Priscilla's company, Miss Kerr gave C.T. some startling news.

'It's not good, Mr Studd. She's getting weaker. I have done everything I can to help her recovery, but she's not responding to it.'

'Is she going to die?'

'I pray she will not. She is just breaking up altogether and can never leave China.'

C.T. exhaled loudly.

'You'd better take her back to England if she can get through this,' recommended Miss Kerr.

'We will give our lives out here willingly!' replied C.T. 'We will not go home unless the Lord distinctly sends us home.' He paced around the room and, in the quietness of his mind, he shot an arrow prayer heavenward: *Lord, please hear my prayer and heal my wife. We trust you completely. You are so faithful to us.*

Turning to Miss Kerr, C.T. announced his intention to anoint his wife with oil and pray for healing. By the grace of God, the next morning Priscilla was well recovered. The little band of missionaries gave thanks to the Lord for his mercy and goodness. It wasn't long before Priscilla was back on her feet and back to work, looking after Grace and caring for anyone who needed her help in the opium refuge.

C. T. Studd

The Studd family grew in the early 1890s with the addition of three more daughters. Dorothy, Edith, and Pauline were born about a year apart from each other. The girls thrived in a loving home, learning about Jesus from their parents and witnessing for themselves the Christian love their parents had for their Chinese neighbours.

Still, the frequency and intensity of childbirth, and the challenges and strains of ministry in China began to take their toll on Priscilla and C.T.'s health. His asthma had worsened from the smoke-filled rooms in which he ministered to his tobacco-loving Chinese neighbours. In the Spring of 1893, C.T. was so ill he felt the Lord was going to take him to heaven. But he rallied his strength and improved. Priscilla and the girls were spared from the sorrow of losing him.

Was it time to go home? they wondered. The family prayed long and hard about it until they felt at peace with the decision to return to England.

C.T. had spent ten years in China serving the Lord Jesus. Now he was going home to his mother in Hyde Park Gardens, with a wife and four children, none of whom she had met.

Life's full of challenges, he chuckled to himself.

The Mission to India

In the sitting room of Hyde Park Gardens in London, Mrs Studd's four granddaughters stood at attention in front of her as she studied their angelic faces .

'They don't understand a word of English?' she asked her son.

'Not a word,' C.T. confirmed, glancing sideways at Priscilla who was perched on an elegantly ornate green chaise-longue next to him.

'Why did you not teach them any English?'

'No one spoke English in Lungan-Fu, mother dearest. Scilla and I thought it best to fully immerse them in the local language and culture.'

The girls smiled at their grandmother as if on cue.

'Well, now it's time to immerse them into our language and culture, Charles.'

'Of course, mother.'

In Chinese, C.T. dismissed the girls, encouraging them to go and play in the garden. They scurried out of the room and started giggling loudly when they reached the hallway. They had never been on parade before. Their giggles made Priscilla smile. She wanted to giggle too, but thought her mother-in-law would not approve.

From Cricket to Christ

'I have appointed a nanny for Pauline and nursemaid for the other three girls. I am sure you will agree that this will prove beneficial for them as they settle in here. It will ease the burden from you and Priscilla as you get your strength back.'

It was welcome news. The four girls were lively, no doubt about that, and their parents appreciated the help for the time being. The children provided the extended family with many memorable occasions around the dinner table over the ensuing months, jabbering to the family in broken English and Chinese, and receiving roars of laughter from their uncles and aunts. It was all in good fun.

C.T. viewed his coming back to the West as simply a change in battleground for the souls of many. As he grew stronger, he arranged speaking engagements across Britain. His preaching tour was then extended to America, where in 1896 he began a visit which lasted eighteen months, in which he went around proclaiming the gospel to thousands of people. Wherever he appeared, there was never a church building or a hall empty. It was said of him that 'he preached Christ as though he would never preach again, and as a dying man to dying men[1].'

As a young Christian, he hoped that one day the Lord would allow him to travel to Tirhoot in Northern India where his father, Edward Studd, had made his

---

1. *Reluctant Missionary*, by Edith Buxton (Hodder and Stoughton, London, 1968) page 31.

C.T. Studd

fortune from his indigo plantations. C.T. wanted to bring the good news about Jesus Christ to the people there; it was his father's dying wish that the people of Tirhoot should hear the gospel from a Studd.

The opportunity came when a friend of his father's encouraged C.T. to go to India. He would make all the arrangements. Once there, C.T. could hold meetings among the planters and preach the gospel. There were wonderful opportunities for the spread of the gospel in India – how could the missionary refuse?

Leaving Priscilla and the four girls at Hyde Park Gardens, C.T. travelled to India in 1900. India had been governed by Britain since 1858 and as a result, Anglo-Indian communities had sprung up, most of whose lineage was paternally English and maternally Indian.

C.T. spent six months preaching the gospel around the plantations in northern Tirhoot. It was during this time that he became aware of the missionary work of the Anglo-Indian Evangelization Society. Formed in England around 1870, the society's purpose was to appoint evangelists who would visit towns and cities in India and exhort all Churches and Missions, and anyone who understood and spoke English, to live for Christ. Especially, these evangelists would seek out the widely scattered European and Anglo-Indian people of the country, and tell them the good news about Jesus and his love.

Travelling to the southern districts of Madras and Mysore, the missionary continued to talk to people

81

From Cricket to Christ

about Jesus Christ, encouraging them to repent and place their trust in him. C.T.'s work also took him into the town of Ootacamund, or Ooty as it was called, in the Madras district.

Union Church was a small independent church in Ooty town. It was known locally as the 'Tin Tabernacle' because a lot of tin was used in its construction. It was under the patronage of the Anglo-Indian Evangelization Society, which meant that the society could appoint a pastor when the position was vacant. When they asked C.T. to be the pastor of Union Church, it was an offer he gladly accepted. Now that he had secured a position that provided a home and a living allowance to cover expenses, C.T. sent for his family in England to join him in India.

Ooty was populated by a number of English people who had relocated there for work. They were known as expatriates, or expats, as they were people who lived outside their own country for a period of time. The expats were just as much in need of hearing the gospel of Jesus Christ as the rest of the indigenous population of India.

During a portion of the year, C.T. ministered to the congregation of Union Church in Ooty, and the remainder of the year he devoted his work among the planters in the surrounding districts of Nilgiris and Travancore.

Naturally C.T. needed very little introduction among expats at Ooty, as most were fully aware of his marvellous cricketing accomplishments when he was a young athlete. And there happened to be a cricket club of sorts which played matches in an area of land, known as a gymkhana, given over to sports. It was the perfect opportunity to use his cricketing expertise to open doors of communication among the young British soldiers stationed in the area, many of whom loved a good game of cricket.

Cricket matches were played every week, and it wasn't long before C.T. regained some of the excellent form he'd had before leaving England for his mission work in China. Players and spectators alike were treated to incredible performances from England's greatest all-round cricketer.

When the games were over, C.T. often invited the young men, some of them army officers, back to his home for refreshments and a conversation about Jesus Christ, conversations which could last long into the night. Sometimes guests were allowed to kip on the couch if the conversation flowed into the wee hours.

One morning, Edith and Dorothy entered the sitting room and stopped suddenly in their tracks. Edith pointed to the sofa. 'There's another one,' she whispered. A young man was extended the length of the couch, on his back, his snores loudly reverberating off the ceiling.

'Maybe mother will let us off piano practice this morning?' wondered Dorothy. 'We certainly don't want to wake our visitor.'

From Cricket to Christ

'You're absolutely right. I'll be back in a moment,' Edith said softly as she disappeared into the kitchen where Priscilla was making breakfast.

A moment later, Edith appeared and stood next to Dorothy. 'Mother says it was time he was awake, and we should start our practice. Perhaps that will do the trick.'

The girls tiptoed softly to the piano in the corner of the room. There was a playful mischief in their eyes. Suddenly, the cacophony of sound erupted from the piano as the girls gleefully hammered the keys. They chuckled as they saw their slumbering guest propelled into the upright position on the sofa in a state of confusion and fear that he was under attack from something or someone noisy!

Priscilla appeared quickly in the entrance to the room, hands on hips. 'Girls!' she exclaimed in a tone of chastisement.

The reply came in unison. 'Sorry, Mother.' They turned to their victim. 'Sorry, sir.'

'That's quite alright, girls. You definitely got me!' he cheerfully replied, now that he was fully awake.

The girls thought the soldiers of the army base were always good fun.

C.T. walked into the room. 'Good morning, girls!' he chirped. He looked at the young soldier. 'You still here?' he said playfully. 'Would you like some breakfast?'

'No thank you, Padre, I have to go,' replied the soldier. He quickly got up, politely bade his farewells to the girls and Mrs Studd, then hurried out the door.

C. T. Studd

'Something I said?' C.T. asked the girls who burst out laughing.

'You're funny, Daddy!' chirped Dorothy.

'What would you say if, after breakfast, I hitch Billie up to the cart and we all go for a ride?' C.T. suggested exuberantly. Looking out the sitting room window, he added, 'Seems like a nice morning for it.'

'Yes please, Daddy!' shrieked Edith. 'We'll tell the others.' The girls ran out of the room excitedly to find their sisters.

It was a regular activity for the Studds to harness their horse Billie to the buggy cart and go for a ride up and down the surrounding hills and pastures of Ooty. These outings were a white-knuckled adventure for the girls who hung on for dear life to the edges of the cart, as Billie attacked the narrow winding cobble-stoned routes with majestic vigour. C.T.'s driving was masterful, of course, and he enjoyed the entertainment his daughters provided along the way as they squealed and laughed in terror and awe of Billie's power on the road. The Studd girls loved a good thrill, were afraid of nothing, and were curious about everything, just as their father had reared them to be.

One day, at the end of a church service in the Tin Tabernacle, Edith's curiosity got the better of her. As the congregation milled around and chatted, she stealthily crept towards the box that held the Communion wine, making sure no one saw where she was going. She had never had Communion wine before

85

From Cricket to Christ

and wondered what it was like. She lifted the lid of the beautifully polished mahogany box and peeked inside.

'What are you doing, Miss Edith?'

The voice startled her. She let go of the lid. It slammed shut. Edith turned to see the churchwarden standing behind her, peering down at her as he waited patiently for her answer. He looked mildly amused at the situation.

'Nothing,' replied Edith innocently.

'You're wondering about the wine,' he said to her.

'What does it taste like?' she asked.

He answered, 'Perhaps you will find out one day.'

'Maybe I'll ask father about it.'

'That would be a good idea.'

Edith skipped to her mother who was standing with a small group of visitors, all of whom were chatting about the sermon they had heard from C.T. during the morning's service. She took Priscilla by the hand and stood quietly next to her. Edith wasn't listening to the conversation. She was deep in thought, wondering when a good time would be to ask her father about Communion…and the wine.

Edith tuned into the conversation and heard her mother say to one of the visitors, 'I beg your pardon?'

'It's true. As we were walking past this little church, our guide pointed to the building and said, "That place is to be avoided unless a man means to get converted."'

'Well, do you?' asked Priscilla. 'Do you mean to get converted?'

C. T. Studd

'I already am, Madam. I have known Christ my Saviour and Lord for many years,' the gentleman replied. 'And, having listened to your husband today, I can understand why the guide said what he did!'

'Some think my husband is very forthright, that is true. But it is also true that no one knows when the Lord Jesus shall return, and it is the mission of his church to tell people to be ready to meet him when he does.'

'Well said, Mrs Studd,' the gentleman agreed.

Edith loosed her mother's hand and went to find Dorothy. She reckoned the grown-ups would be chatting for a wee while yet. Her father loved to see people staying to talk with each other after a church meeting. It was a great opportunity for them to encourage each other in the faith of Christ. He didn't think it was right for people to come into church, sit on their own, not talk to anyone, and then leave without a word when the service was over. True believers didn't behave like that, he'd say. Serve the Lord and serve each other in love, he'd say.

Finally the opportunity came for Edith to ask her father about Holy Communion. There was strength in numbers, so she waited until her sisters were with her to back her up.

'Father, we think we are ready to take Holy Communion,' Edith declared.

'Do you?' replied her father.

'Yes, we do. So when can we start?'

'Well that's a good question, Edith.'

From Cricket to Christ

Edith smiled. Father thought she had asked a good question.

C.T. continued, 'But I will have to ask you all some questions about your faith in Jesus Christ.'

The girls nodded. C.T. then quizzed them to find out what each of them believed about Jesus Christ and most importantly if each girl personally knew Jesus as Saviour and Lord. He was so satisfied with their responses that when the spiritual examination was over, he joyfully exclaimed, 'Every one of you must be baptised in the name of Jesus Christ!'

Plans were made for the girls to be baptised as soon as the baptismal tank was prepared in the garden. A large hole was dug and lined with tin to hold the water.

The rain fell hard in Ooty on the day the girls were baptised in the garden, but it did not dampen their spirits. The whole congregation of Union Church had been invited to watch the ceremony, to give thanks to God for the children's faith in Jesus Christ, and to rejoice with those who rejoiced[2].

As parents, C.T. and Priscilla were proud of their children. Saved by Jesus and heaven bound, joy and peace filled the hearts of this little family in India.

After six years in Ooty, it was time for C.T. and his family to return to England. The climate wasn't great for someone who suffered from asthma as badly as C.T. did. Priscilla described him as a 'wreck' – not good. Plus,

---

2. Romans 12:15.

the girls needed an education the leverl of which wasn't available in the town.

In 1906 the Studds boarded a boat bound for England. Mission in India may have been over, but for Charles it was simply a matter of asking, 'What's next, Lord?'

Cannibals Want Missionaries

The children's stay with Granny at Hyde Park Gardens in London was short-lived. Dorothy, Edith and Grace were sent to a boarding school in Lausanne, Switzerland to make up for the lack of education that was available to them in Ooty. Pauline was too young to go.

On a mild autumn morning in 1906, Priscilla stood on the platform at Victoria station in London and watched the train slowly pull away from the station. She raised a hand of farewell to her girls as they hung out the window sorrowfully waving 'goodbye' to their tearful mother. It was a new adventure for them, paid for by their wealthy aunt Dora and her husband, Willie Bradshaw.

Rest and recuperation may have been the doctor's orders, but C.T. would not prolong his absence from preaching the gospel in England. News of his return quickly spread, and invitations to preach at venues across the country flooded in. The moment he was able, C.T. started to accept the numerous offers to speak at various events.

The multitudes were drawn by his sporting reputation. Thousands of people flocked to hear the words of the finest cricketer England had ever

91

From Cricket to Christ

produced. Curiously, he did not speak of his sport, or of his family's wealth nor success. He did not seek to motivate his listeners to be innovative entrepreneurs. He spoke only of Jesus Christ and the salvation the Lord came to bring each of his hearers. He challenged Christians to proclaim Christ fearlessly to the lost before it was too late and they took up residence in hell forever.

One day C.T. was invited to have lunch with a group of local businessmen. It was a great opportunity to preach to them the gospel of Christ, so he went. It was a fine feast, and they ate as much as they wanted. As soon as the meal was over, C.T. stood to address his gastronomically content audience.

'Gentlemen, you've had a rich dinner, and now you will be ready for plain speaking,' he began. 'I am not going to tickle you with a pulpit or academic display of language. I shall speak ordinary language, one in which we are all accustomed to use when engaged in the real battle of life, or in heart-to-heart talking. I once had another religion: mincing, lisping, bated breath, proper, hunting the Bible for hidden truths, but no obedience or sacrifice. Then came the change. The real thing came before me. The commands of Christ became not merely Sunday recitations, but battle calls to be obeyed. I began to look upon God as really my Father, and to rely upon Him as a real Father, and to trust Him as such. Instead of talking about fellowship, I enjoyed it. I talked of God and Jesus Christ as real, living, personal

92

friends and relations. They have never chided me for it. If a man is willing to obey and sacrifice, he soon learns what is the blessed reality of the fellowship of God's Son, Jesus Christ. In other words, I dropped insincerity, ceremony, and tradition, and became a Christian. Reverence, I observe in the New Testament, is not apparent politeness and clear disobedience, but childlike obedience, trust, and love.'

He spoke plainly, at times with humour, and this appealed to his listeners. During the course of his time in England, many people came to love and trust Christ personally through hearing the gospel from C.T. Studd. Even newspaper reporters that were inclined to be cynical of preachers could not help but admire his moxy.

Following a meeting in Handsworth, an area in inner city Birmingham, a local newspaper commented,

> 'Mr Studd is a missionary to emulate. And so all that band of college men from Handsworth thought as they cheered him to the echo, this man with the red tie and slim athletic body and the young face. After more than twenty years of harness he is bubbling over with life and humour; no pessimism about him, no lukewarmness; he loves and he follows, he teaches what he believes, he keeps a brave sunshiny face through all. No subtleties appear to puzzle him; his faith is as brave as his speech is clear and straight.[1]

---

1. *C.T. Studd, Cricketer and Pioneer*, by Norman P. Grubb (The Lutterworth Press, Cambridge, 1933) page 108.

From Cricket to Christ

But it was a trip to Liverpool that fired the missionary's zeal for the continent of Africa. As he was walking down a street in the city, C.T. saw the most curious sign outside a building. It read, 'Cannibals want missionaries'.

I'm sure they do, for more reasons than one! C.T. chuckled to himself. Intrigued as to who would write such a sign, he nipped inside to investigate. He found a large room filled with people and joined the back row.

A hefty man with a thick German accent was speaking. His name was Dr Karl Kumm, the founder of the Sudan United Mission. Having recently returned from walking across Africa, Dr Kumm was relaying his experiences to the attentive crowd before him. He reported that there were many African tribes that were still ignorant of Jesus Christ. People from all walks of life, from all over the world, had trekked through Africa, but no Christian had ever gone to tell the people about Jesus Christ. And this spiritual crisis was being intensified by the advance of Islam through many African regions.

Oh the shame! thought C.T. *What possible excuse could be given in defence of such a travesty?* He often wondered why Christians in England were so tame, so domesticated. *Too comfortable*, he concluded.

As Dr Kumm's stories of Africa filled the air, in the quietness of his own mind, C.T. turned to prayer to enquire of the Lord. Immediately he felt the challenge

C. T. Studd

to go to Africa himself, trusting in the Great Physician to strengthen him and keep him for the task. No doubt his doctor would caution against travelling to the tropical climes of Africa. It simply wouldn't be good for his health.

He thought of the special women in his life. They may object too. Priscilla and the girls could not follow him there this time. Apart from a loving wife's desire to keep C.T. safe and well – she had watched him struggle for so many years with asthma – Priscilla's own health problems would not allow for rigorous trekking through the jungles of Africa. On top of that, a quickly caught tropical disease could easily speed her demise.

Also, the girls were growing up, and were starting to make their own way in the world. They had been in Lausanne for less than two years, returning to England to continue their education in Sherborne School in Sherborne, Dorset. And it wouldn't be too many years before marriage and family life would come calling.

His dearest mother would simply want her loving son in London, close by so she could keep a protective eye on him.

Nonetheless, the Africans needed Jesus Christ. And on their wedding day, Mr and Mrs Studd promised never to get in the way of each other's service of the Lord. That settled it. Dr Kumm and C.T. arranged a meeting to talk about mission in Africa. Dr Kumm suggested an initial trip to Africa for the two men.

From Cricket to Christ

C.T. could get the lay of the land and have a better understanding of the spiritual challenges that faced a Christian missionary there.

Dr Kumm pointed out that Central Africa was untouched by the gospel of Christ. The need to start a Christian mission in the Congo was immense.

The Congo Free State was established in 1885 by the king of Belgium, Leopold II, who added the region to his personal portfolio. He financed development projects there through money loaned to him by the Belgian government. King Leopold let it be known that he intended to bring 'civilisation' to the tribal people of the Congo, but his reign over the Congolese was notorious for its brutality. He used the local people to extract valuable resources from the land, such as rubber and ivory, and he grew exceedingly wealthy. Under Leopold's reign, the people were worked too hard and suffered from malnutrition and disease, and many were tortured. Not surprisingly huge numbers of people died.

Rebellions against King Leopold were promptly and ferociously squashed. However, it was impossible to keep the lid on such abuses, and when news of the injustices reached Europe, demonstrations, protests, and political pressure forced Leopold II to turn the Congo Free State over to the Belgian government. It was then renamed in 1908 as the 'Belgian Congo'.

As predicted, the tears flowed when C.T. announced his desire to set up a mission in Africa. His mother was more open about her dislike of his decision than his wife. Instead, Priscilla took to weeping quietly at the thought of her physically frail, middle-aged husband going to deepest darkest Africa.

Dr Kumm made the trip alone. C.T. was suffering from malaria and was in no fit state to go anywhere. The family were glad to have him stay in England, even though it was the unfortunate circumstance of illness that kept him there.

But it was only a temporary reprieve for them. As he grew stronger, C.T. mustered up a group of supportive businessmen to back his plan to pioneer a new mission in the heart of Africa. They agreed to fund his efforts if his doctors gave him a full bill of health.

There was the rub! The doctor was definitely not backing C.T.'s excursion to Africa on medical grounds. He simply was not well enough. The doctor told him that if he went out, he would not come back.

Undeterred, a trip to Southern Sudan was scheduled for a few weeks away.

Unfortunately, the small committee of businessmen decided not to support C.T.'s mission trip to Africa. He immediately wrote a terse but polite response to them: 'Gentlemen, God has called me to go, and I will go. I will blaze the trail, though my grave may only become a stepping stone that younger men may follow.'

The words of Jesus, his Lord and Saviour, were at the forefront of his mind: 'For whoever would save his

From Cricket to Christ

life will lose it, but whoever loses his life for my sake will find it.'[2]

It didn't matter to C.T. that he had no money or backing. All he wanted to do was obey God and bring the glorious gospel of the Saviour to the heart of Africa. He believed that if God was for it, no one would stop him.

The next day C.T. had a speaking engagement in Birmingham, England. The folks who had gathered to hear him preach were unaware of his disappointments, only that he was set to sail for Africa soon.

Trusting in God for the finances, C.T. addressed the crowd as though he were still sailing, and he never mentioned the setbacks he had recently encountered. He went next to Liverpool and spoke at a series of events that had been lined up for the weekend. He said nothing of the withdrawal of support from his small business committee or his doctor, and he would never mention the lack of support of his darling Priscilla.

Prompted by the Holy Spirit, a newly-made friend thrust some money into C.T.'s hand to help with any mission expenses. The missionary could not curtail his joy and excitement. He praised the Lord – the trip to Africa was on!

C.T. set sail from the English port of Liverpool on the 15th of December 1910. His destination was Khartoum in Sudan. The plan was then to trek a thousand miles south of Khartoum, and investigate the spiritual plight

2. Matthew 16:25.

C.T. Studd

of Southern Sudan. That first night on board in his cabin, C.T. felt as if the Lord was preparing him for a mission to the whole unevangelised world. He had absolutely no idea how this marvellous vision would come to pass. But Jesus laughs at impossibilities, he thought.

The voyage gave him plenty of time to write letters home. It was a good opportunity to help Priscilla understand his heart, and perhaps to soften hers to his mission for Jesus. Five days out to sea, he sat at a little writing table in his cabin, and started writing letters to his beloved.

> Scilla darling, all this separation is for our good, and what is far better, it is for God's glory and Christ's honour. I believe this assuredly: (1) Your health shall be restored. (2) You shall become a bigger firebrand for Jesus than ever you have been, and a far greater power than poor, weak I could ever be. (3) Our girls shall be white-hot Christian warriors, and to God be all the glory. I think and think and think, and all upon the same line – A New Crusade. Things simply surge through my mind and head, and God speaks to me every time I lie down, and assures me that He is going to do a wonderful work… The doctors would have frightened me into my grave long ago had I paid attention to them, but I live, and live by faith in Jesus and the power of God. You must do the same. I am going forward, trusting in Him. There are big things ahead. Join with me in this Crusade…God bless you, darling.[3]

---

3. *C.T. Studd, Cricketer and Pioneer,* by Norman P. Grubb (The Lutterworth Press, Cambridge, 1933) pages 114-115.

From Cricket to Christ

From Khartoum to Southern Sudan, C.T. was accompanied by the Anglican Bishop of Khartoum, Llewellyn Henry Gwynne and Archdeacon Archibald Shaw of the Church Missionary Society.[4] It was a challenging journey for the men and mules who embarked on the long trek. The going was difficult and slow, through disease-infected plains of the Bahr-el-Ghazal, a region named after the western tributary that flowed to the Nile.

The Church Missionary Society had been operating in Sudan since 1900 and C.T. felt that another new mission would only get in the way of their work for the Lord in that area. What really interested C.T. was the information his group had received during their trek, of vast numbers of deprived and depraved people living in the Belgian Congo who had never heard anything about Jesus Christ.

The new crusade became clear in his mind. C.T. would not return to England to stay. God wanted him in the Congo.

---

4. The Church Missionary Society was formed in 1799 by a group of evangelical clergy and laity of the Church of England under the chair of John Venn, rector of Holy Trinity Church, Clapham, England.

Journey to the Heart of Africa

A sudden burst of rain forced the men to take cover in their tents which they had pitched close to the lake shore. They hadn't thought much about the dangers in the water either, until the crocodiles made their presence known with their loud grunting noises. C.T. decided it was prudent to keep the fire lit throughout the night if possible, to deter any hungry snapping reptiles from paying them a visit under the cover of darkness.

The sun rose on the intrepid missionaries shortly after 5 a.m. They packed up and headed for the nearest government outpost. As predicted, the Belgian officials were so impressed, but more likely tickled by their broken French, they warmly welcomed the two men into the territory of the Belgian Congo. They were even provided with some porters to assist them on their journey into the dense, wooded heartland of the Congo where it would be easy to lose their sense of direction.

The way ahead was fraught with danger. The Balenda tribe was feared by other tribes in the Congo for their brutality, and the missionaries would have to pass through their area.

From Cricket to Christ

'You'll never come through alive,' one of the traders said before the men left the outpost.

'They'll be too interested in our bicycles to do anything to us,' C.T. jovially replied.

'Bicycles!' exclaimed the trader in astonishment. 'So you mean to say you are going to bicycle through the jungle?'

'Certainly,' C.T. replied. 'We'll get to the other end more quickly. And when the bicycles can't carry us, we'll carry them.'

Off they went through the African bush, riding their bikes when they could, and carrying them over rough jungle terrain when they couldn't.

Not long into the expedition the missionaries discovered that they had travelled too far away from their helpers.

'Can you hear the porters?' C.T. called to Alfred from the back of his bike. They slammed on the brakes and listened intently.

'I can't hear anything,' replied Alfred.

'Let's try to find them,' C.T. suggested.

They peddled back as quick as the track would let them. But the porters were nowhere to be found. They were lost in the African jungle. For three hours the missionaries trekked up and down steep hills, and through villages densely-populated by different Congolese tribes, but they could not find their helpers. The bicycles were more of a hindrance than a help as they had to be carried for much of the search. To top

C. T. Studd

it all, they had no food, no money, and no knowledge of the language.

All of a sudden, they heard the snap of twigs from the bushes. When they looked in the direction of the noise, they saw a partially-dressed African man standing perfectly still. He was looking at them in a curious manner. The sight of two quintessential Englishmen in knickerbockers[1] holding bicycles, in the middle of his jungle, undoubtedly surprised him. And then it seemed to amuse him slightly. He smiled, revealing a mouth full of teeth that had been filed to sharp points: he was a cannibal. Alfred swallowed hard and tried to appear calm. He could see that the man carried a basket filled with corn and sweet potatoes in one hand, and a bow and some arrows in the other.

The three men stared at each other for what seemed like an eternity. Eventually C.T. stepped towards the man, who in turn moved a step backwards. C.T. pointed at the basket of food and then at his own very empty stomach. Alfred nodded and did the same thing. He was hungry too.

The sign language did the trick. The basket was held up for the starving men to take what they needed.

The missionaries successfully traded for the food with what little possessions they had on them at the time. Their jumgle visitor was happy to accept even small things like buttons in exchange. CT and the others

---

1. Knickerbockers are loose-fitting trousers that are gathered in at the knee.

From Cricket to Christ

were thankful as they had no money – and money would have been of no use in the jumgle either.

They pressed on northeast to the gold-mining region of Kilo but were stranded there for a few months, partly because of a lack of helpers to assist them further into the heart of the country, but also because it was the wet season. The jungle rains were frequent and rigorous. C.T. fell sick with a terrible bout of fever. At one point he thought he was close to death, but God restored his servant to health.

When the time came to leave Kilo, Alfred and C.T. trekked for eleven days through the huge tropical forest of Ituri, the tall, lush green trees majestically lining their path as they headed deeper and deeper into the Congo. This place was home to the African forest people known as Pygmies, so-called because of their short stature.

The missionaries then came to Dungu town where they met the Belgian District Commissioner who welcomed them like long-lost friends. He made sure the men were looked after while they were in his company. They were grateful for his hospitality. The commissioner granted them access to the luxurious grassland locations of Niangara and Nala, places which were filled with people who had never heard the gospel of Jesus Christ. The weary travellers were excited to get there.

After nine months of gruelling travels, they had finally reached their destination. Alfred Buxton

C.T. Studd

and C.T. Studd arrived in Niangara on the 16th of October, 1913.

The Heart of Africa Mission (H.A.M.) was born.

The Mission in Africa

The Mission in Africa

Nine months of living in tents were close to an end. C.T. and Alfred found a suitable plot in Niangara and were given permission by the government and the local chief to build a house. They gathered thin and flexible long branches from the forest and stripped any leaves off them. Then, they took the branches and wove them between stronger wooden posts which had been driven into the ground. Finally, they cemented the structure together with mud. It was a palace compared to the flimsy accommodation in which they had lived in during their wet and arduous trek there, so C.T. humorously called the first mission house 'Buckingham Palace' after the luxurious London palace of the British monarchy.

A five-day trip south of Niangara took the missionaries to the beautiful setting of Nala. The region was densely populated with people, and the men believed it to be a good location for a second mission station. It was clear to them that they could push further out from Nala into the surrounding forest and meet more Congolese tribes to tell them the good news about Jesus and his love.

The town of Poko and Bambili, northwest of Nala, became the sites of the third and fourth mission stations

From Cricket to Christ

of the Heart of Africa Mission, the name C.T. bestowed upon the gospel endeavour while in the Belgian Congo. The four new mission stations covered an area half the size of England and encompassed ten different tribes.

Alfred and C.T worked hard to become fluent in Bangala, the local language. It was a language that the tribes used to trade with each other. Thankfully, Bangala wasn't a complicated language, and foreign visitors were able to learn it quite easily to converse with the locals.

From the four mission houses at Niangara, Nala, Poko, and Bambili, the missionaries ventured out into the villages and surrounding areas, frequently on their bicycles, to meet people and proclaim the Word of God to them.

The missionaries were enthusiastically welcomed by villagers who listened to their preaching with joy. Many people repented of their sins and placed their faith in Jesus as Saviour and Lord. Six months after arriving at Nala, there was a baptismal service for eighteen locals.

'Can you imagine what the headline would be in *The War Cry*[1] back home if they knew about this? "Ex-Cannibals, Drunkards, Thieves, Murderers, Adulterers, and Swearers Enter the Kingdom of God,"' said Alfred to C.T. as they watched the people line up by the Congo River to be baptized.

---

1. **The War Cry** is the monthly mission magazine of The Salvation Army. The first issue was published in 1879 in London, England.

C.T. pointed to one of the candidates. 'Do you remember his confession of sin the other evening at the meeting? "I have done more sin than there is room for in my chest."'

Alfred nodded. 'And now look at him. Born again of the Spirit of God and waiting to be baptized in the name of Jesus Christ.'

Back in England, Priscilla and her daughters, Edith and Pauline, worked hard to rally interest and support for the ministry of the Heart of Africa Mission (H.A.M.) in the Belgian Congo. The H.A.M. headquarters was Number 17 Highland Road in Upper Norwood, London. Before he'd left for Africa, C.T. had purchased this ramshackle house for the family after Priscilla pressed him for their own home. The money for the property was gifted to them from C.T.'s mother.

Leaving Alfred to carry on the work in the Congo, C.T. returned to England in 1914 to drum up recruits for the Heart of Africa Mission. He found the headquarters in Upper Norwood a hive of activity: magazines, prayer events, and prolific letter writing were all part of the mission's arsenal for developing partnerships with individuals and churches. Even the Great War[2] that had begun to rage in Europe did not stop the work. He travelled up and down the country appealing for Christian people to join him in the Belgian Congo.

When it was time to return to the Belgian Congo in the summer of 1916, C.T. had eight new missionary

---

2. World War I, 1914-1918.

From Cricket to Christ

recruits. Edith Studd was one of them. Edith had been ""writing letters to Alfred Buxton ever since the last time she saw him over four years ago. Their love and devotion to God and to each other was strong and now they intended to marry…as long as Alfred didn't have a big bushy beard! Imagine Edith's relief when she met him and saw he was clean shaven. The wedding was on.

The service was held at 'Buckingham Palace' in Niangara and was led by Edith's father. The locals crowded in to see the first Christian wedding between two Westerners in the heart of Africa. It was a jubilant occasion, followed by a magnificent jungle feast. However, as C.T. did not belong to a religious denomination and was therefore not an ordained clergyman of the Church of England, the legal service needed to be conducted by an official from the Belgian government.

The wedding party hopped into their canoes and rowed to the government outpost nearby, whereby they were warmly greeted by the Belgian commissioner and other dignitaries. The service lasted only five minutes and the proceedings were completed as the newlyweds signed the marriage certificate. Everyone enjoyed the customary tea and wedding cake, but not so much the garbled French from the missionaries.

The next day, Mr and Mrs Buxton disappeared for a short honeymoon on a beautiful island up-river. Meanwhile, C.T. returned to Nala and made the place H.A.M.'s operational headquarters in the Congo.

C. T. Studd

From Nala, the foreign and native missionaries were sent out to other towns and villages to tell their neighbours the good news of Jesus Christ. The native missionaries carried very little with them on their travels: a grass mat to lie on, a jungle knife and an enamel cup hanging on the belt, and a personally-designed straw hat completed their jungle survival kits.

C.T. penned a report to the H.A.M. headquarters about the evangelistic zeal of the local church. It was dated the 10th of October, 1918.

> The progress is simply wonderful; people are coming to us from every quarter and from very long distances. We are having pretty nearly weekly baptisms. The converts are evangelising far and near. Many chiefs are imploring us to send them teachers and are even building chapels and houses for us… Four men came a 20 days' journey to Nala, and when asked why, said, "All the world knows there is much knowledge of God at Nala."

Not only that, boarding schools for girls and boys were set up at opposite ends of the village with fifty students in each. God was clearly blessing the ministry of his faithful people in the Belgian Congo.

During church services, C.T. led everyone in singing hymns of praise to God on his banjo. He had learned to play the instrument at Eton. The congregation enthusiastically sang songs that were written by D.L. Moody and Ira Sankey, and translated into Bangala for them. On occasion there were 'testimony' meetings,

From Cricket to Christ

where people told their stories of how they became followers of Jesus Christ.

'What's he saying?' Edith softly asked Alfred one evening, as a man was giving a testimony that appeared to captivate the assembly.

'He's just told us that he is sorry he has to confess that he has eaten his uncle,' replied Alfred matter-of-factly.

Edith squirmed at the thought, even though she was absolutely convinced that the man had sincerely repented of his sins and turned to Christ for forgiveness. 'And God is faithful and just to forgive us our sins and to cleanse us from all unrighteousness,'[3] she reminded herself.

The consensus amongst the new H.A.M. missionaries was that nothing could have prepared them for the realities of life in the African jungle. They adapted well to the lack of home comforts and possessions that Westerners were accustomed to, but the perpetual bouts of malaria and other fevers, which plagued most missionaries during their service in the mission field, were hard. Edith noticed that it was taking her father longer to recover from each attack of fever that he suffered.

In 1918 the Buxton's, now a family of three due to the birth of baby Susan, left Africa for a much needed break in England. Susan was nine months old when she experienced the mild English climate for the first

3. 1 John 1:9.

time, not to mention seeing her great-grandmother Mrs Studd in London. The Buxton's were joined by four other missionaries, also requiring a good rest. The group's departure left the mission in the Congo severely depleted in personnel, as the Great War had prevented others from coming out to join the work in the heart of Africa for the time being. It was going to be a challenge for C.T. to keep on top of the volume of work given his frequent attacks of fever and his frail health. But he fully trusted that if the Lord had a work for him, then the Lord would absolutely strengthen him to do it.

At the London headquarters, Priscilla mustered the members of the H.A.M. Committee to fervent prayer. She often heard her husband say that prayer is good, but when it is used as a substitute for obedience it is nothing but a blatant hypocrisy. They begged God for prayerful and obedient servants of Christ who would go to the mission's frontline. This prayer was answered swiftly, as a small group of new recruits set sail for the Belgian Congo in 1920. It included their youngest daughter Pauline. She had married Norman Grubb, the son of an Irish Anglican clergyman, in the winter of the previous year.

The Heart of Africa Mission was certainly a family affair. Dorothy's husband, Mr Gilbert Barclay, got involved as its Home Overseer, helping Mrs Studd direct the work of the Heart of Africa Mission in the British Isles. Gilbert's vision for the mission was

From Cricket to Christ

greater than Africa. He wanted the boundaries of mission activity to be pushed into other continents, such as South America. With that in mind, a change of name was suggested and adopted by the Committee. The mission would now become the Worldwide Evangelization Crusade.

There was never an appeal for money for the Crusade at any meeting or event. It would continue as it started, by trusting completely in the one who told his followers not to be anxious about anything, but rather, 'seek first the kingdom of God and his righteousness, and all these things will be added to you.'[4]

Towards the end of the Buxtons' furlough in England, Lionel Buxton was born. Susan was a toddler and enjoying life in London surrounded by her extended family who simply adored her. However, Alfred and Edith felt the need to return to the Congo. In the winter of 1921, Susan and Lionel were left in the capable and loving care of Alfred's parents, due to some health issues that would make it unbearable for them in the African jungle.

C.T. was thrilled to have two of his daughters serving Christ with him in the Congo. He felt it was a special privilege for him. Such a great joy and comfort it was to him, knowing all his daughters loved Jesus and would spend eternity with him in heaven.

Now that Alfred had returned, C.T's focus turned to the dense tropical Ituri rainforest which lay a four

4. Matthew 6:33.

114

day's trek south of Nala. He planned to leave Alfred and Edith to look after the work at Nala while he searched for the Bambuti Pygmies of the Ituri Province to tell them about the love of Jesus Christ.

The large and populous village of Ibambi in the Ituri forest was named after its chief. As C.T. rode in on his bicycle, he saw impeccably crafted bamboo huts which lined the way to the centre of the village. The people came out to catch a glimpse of the Englishman passing by. Some ran alongside him, singing and laughing as they accompanied him to the chief's hut. It seemed like a happy place. But years of experience told C.T. that real life in Ibambi was not filled with joy. Beneath the façade of mirth lay dark secrets of witchcraft, abuse, and crippling fear.

The Bible says, 'The reason the Son of God appeared was to destroy the works of the devil,'[5] C.T. thought to himself, and the devil is hard at work here. I will point them to Jesus Christ. The Holy Spirit will do the rest.

---

5. 1 John 3:8

Bwana Mukubwa

C.T. could hear the people coming from miles around as the beautiful, melodious singing of hymns praising God filled the air, drowning out the bird-song of the rainforest. They came in droves to be taught the Word of God and to be baptized. Women and men, girls and boys from the Ituri Province, all eager to hear Bwana Mukubwa tell them about Jesus and his love. The gospel went out from the mission's new headquarters at Ibambi like concentric rings formed from a pebble plopped into a puddle.

Invitations to teach the Bible arrived from neighbouring villages. Imbai's settlement lay five hours from Ibambi. The people there were hungry for the gospel. C.T.'s heart was moved when he saw 1500 of them sitting tightly together under the noonday sun, each waiting patiently to hear God's voice as God's Word was faithfully brought to them.

Eventually the locals erected a building the size of a cricket pitch that could seat over a thousand people, where they could meet whatever the weather and be edified by the Word of God and where they could encourage one another in the love of Christ.

From Cricket to Christ

C.T. adamantly resisted calls from home which begged him to return to England due to his poor health. There was far too much to do. News of the 'cricket-pitch church' had spread to the surrounding areas. Other chiefs wanted him to teach God's Word and build more cricket-pitch churches. Bwana Mukubwa was not going to abandon them at their hour of need.

By 1923, forty H.A.M. missionaries were in the Lord's service in the Belgian Congo, allowing for other mission stations to be opened across the Ituri Province. C.T.'s insistence on sacrifice and a frugal lifestyle, in keeping with the people of the Congo, was a struggle for some of them, and they did not stay the course. He was known for his uncompromising and determined leadership, come what may. As a soldier for Christ, it was his ambition and prayer to die on the battlefield for lost souls, not in a comfy bed in London.

It was a different matter for his beloved son-in-law, Alfred. Edith told her father that Alfred had taken seriously ill. A rare tropical disease, which would stay with him for the rest of his life, had infected him. When C.T. saw just how sick Alfred was, he urged them both to go home to England. They obeyed him.

Alfred had spent a total of seventeen years in the heart of Africa speaking to people about the crucified Saviour. Those who had come to saving faith in Jesus loved him for bringing the good news into their villages and sharing it with them. They loved him for his gentle manner, always willing to see both sides of a

118

C. T. Studd

disagreement before offering godly advice. They simply loved this sincere man of God.

Now it was time to say goodbye. The farewell was tearful. There was a mixture of sadness and relief in Edith's heart. But they would pray for and support the work of her father and the mission from home.

The hard work continued in the jungle. C.T. often visited the settlement at Imbai to lead large meetings. As he was getting older and physically weaker, he could no longer ride his bicycle or walk the long distances from Ibambi to other outlying villages. A mandala, or carrying chair, was made for him, although he did not like travelling that way because the rich European traders who came into the Belgian Congo would use lavishly ornate mandalas as an expression of their wealth and superiority over the locals. But it was the only way to get around and see his flock.

If Bwana Mukubwa was coming to Imbai for a service, news spread like wildfire through the jungle villages. His preference was an open air meeting under the exotic palm trees which provided the perfect shade from the baking midday sun. The boom of the prayer drum beckoned the surrounding tribes to gather together to hear the Word of God and sing God's praises. Over two hundred hymns were written by C.T. for the people to sing together, and whichever songs they decided to sing at the meeting he led them enthusiastically on his banjo.

There were extended times of prayer and reading of Scripture in the service, followed by Bwana Mukubwa's

From Cricket to Christ

passionate preaching and pleading for the people before him to repent of their sins and to believe in Christ, following and fighting for him in the battle against the flesh, the world, and the devil. 'This is the path to heaven,' he assured them.

These regular meetings lasted for hours, and no one complained. At the end of each service, the people stood and raised their hands to heaven and declared with one voice, 'God is good. Jesus is coming quickly. Hallelujah!' Then the meeting was over, and the people dispersed to their own homes and villages.

Year after year, C.T. and the other H.A.M. missionaries preached the gospel to every tribe they encountered. The passage of time, constant bouts of sickness, and a busy schedule impacted C.T.'s work but did not stop it. When his teeth began to rot and fall out, some of the missionaries encouraged him to go back to England and get them seen to, as he was unable to eat anything other than soft or liquidised food.

'If God wants me to have some new teeth, he can just easily send me some here,' he said jovially. So God did, prompting an English dentist called Mr Buck to go to the Congo and give Bwana Mukubwa a new set of teeth.

Mr Buck was too old to be considered for missionary service with H.A.M, but that did not matter to him. He sold his dental practice and travelled to the edge of the Belgian Congo. Once he got there he did a bit of

C. T. Studd

dentistry amongst the traders and government officials to earn some more money that would help him get to his final destination of Ibambi, where C.T. lived.

The same morning that Mr Buck travelled by canoe up the river into the heart of Africa, Pauline and Norman Grubb were leaving the Congo to return to England to assist with the work at headquarters.

As Mr Buck's canoe came into view, Norman turned to Pauline and said, 'That chap's not one of ours, is he?'

Pauline squinted in the direction of the oncoming canoe. 'No, I don't think so. I wasn't aware anyone was coming at the moment. I wonder if he's English.'

Norman cupped his hands around his mouth like a megaphone. 'Hello there!' he shouted.

'Hello!' came the reply in English, followed by a frantic wave of the hand.

Norman pointed to the riverbank, indicating the desire to stop and talk with the mysterious traveller. They disembarked and walked a short distance to a small clearing in the forest. Then came the introductions.

'I'm Norman Grubb and this is my wife, Pauline. And you are Mister...?'

'Buck.'

'Are you lost, Mr Buck?' enquired Pauline.

'I hope not!' replied Mr Buck. 'I'm heading to see Mr Charles Thomas Studd. I want to be involved in his mission here.'

'He's my father,' said Pauline. 'Does he know you're coming?'

From Cricket to Christ

'Maybe not. It hasn't been that easy getting in touch with him.'

'No, I suppose it's not that easy, is it?'

Norman said, 'I think it's time for a spot of breakfast. Would you like something to eat?'

'Yes, that would be brilliant. I'm famished.'

After breakfast, the small group spent a few moments in prayer before heading back to the canoes at the river's edge.

'Mrs Grubb, might I have a quiet word?' asked Mr Buck as he pulled her gently to one side. He lowered his voice and said solemnly, 'As you are a daughter of Mr Studd's, I would like to tell you a secret that I have told no one else. I am a dentist by profession. God has sent me into the heart of Africa not only to preach the gospel but also to bring Mr Studd a new set of teeth, and I have brought with me all that is necessary for making and fitting them!'

'You're an answer to prayer, Mr Buck,' Pauline said gleefully. 'New teeth will really help my father eat better and gain a bit of strength. The Lord bless you, Mr Buck!'

The missionaries parted company – Mr Buck further inland, and the Grubbs to England. When Mr Buck arrived at Ibambi, he was led by a group of children to Bwana Mukubwa's circular bamboo hut. C.T. was inside, sitting by his homemade table. An old, worn Bible was in front of him, and he was writing in a book. He was determined to translate the New

C. T. Studd

Testament into Kingwana so that the people could have the Word of God in their own language. He did a similar thing for the tribes in the Welle Province who spoke Bangala.

The children dashed into the hut and excitedly announced that there was someone from Bwana Mukubwa's homeland to see him.

Slowly, C.T. rose from his seat and shuffled outside. Mr Buck was greeted with a semi-toothless grin. 'Hello there, Mister...?'

'Buck. I am so pleased to meet you Mr Studd, and to be here in the Congo. I would like to join your gospel endeavour if I may. However. The first thing God sent me to the Congo to do was your teeth. I'm a dentist, you see.'

With two hands, C.T. grasped Mr Buck's right hand and shook it vigorously. 'Welcome, Mr Buck! Welcome to the heart of Africa!'

The men decided on a time to begin the dental work. C.T. needed to pluck up the fortitude to deal with a dentist. Whatever rotten teeth C.T. had left, Mr Buck removed to make way for a set of pearly white dentures.

'I will blind the locals with these if I smile on a sunny day,' C.T. joked as he looked at Mr Buck's handiwork in a small mirror.

'No need to live only on soup now, Mr Studd. You'll be able to chew anything with these beauties,' said Mr Buck.

From Cricket to Christ

Just fancy God sending a dentist to the heart of Africa to look after the teeth of his child who could not return home, C.T. thought. What wonder will God do next?

C.T. found the new teeth a challenge as they rested on sore and healing gums. He couldn't keep them in for too long during services. Old Bwana Mukubwa with a full set of white teeth took some getting used to, but when he rose from prayer with no teeth in his mouth, the look of alarm on his congregation was funny to him. 'Who nicked Bwana's teeth during prayer?!' seemed to be written all over their faces.

New teeth and an improved diet didn't arrest his physical decline. Aware that his health was failing, C.T. worked harder to translate the Scriptures into Kingwana. He did not want to leave his people without the written Word of God.

By 1928, C.T. managed to translate the New Testament, the Psalms, and even some of the book of Proverbs before repeated heart attacks took him close to death's door. Exceedingly strong opioid medication helped him get off his bed and enabled him to keep working. He was grateful for the strength to do a little bit more ministry for the glory of God and the advancement of his kingdom in the heart of Africa.

With the global production of cars, roads were now cut through the interior of the Congo, making it easier for C.T. to call at the mission houses in the Welles and

C.T. Studd

Ituri Provinces. It also meant that Priscilla could visit her husband at Ibambi.

The excitement in the village was palpable because Mama Bwana was coming. They knew Bwana Mukubwa's wife was back in England encouraging people to come to them and tell them about the love of Jesus.

Priscilla was received like royalty when she arrived by car at Ibambi. Two thousand local Christians gathered to welcome Mama Bwana into their midst. She looked so much younger than her husband, almost young enough to be his daughter!

The visit lasted two short weeks, during which time the Studds were watched closely. The people loved to hear Mama Bwana speak to them about Jesus, the lilt of her beautiful Northern Irish accent making her words sound so lovely, and so funny.

Everyone could see the devotion and tenderness that C.T. and Priscilla had for each other. No one doubted the immense sacrifice these two servants of Christ had made in bringing the message of salvation to the Congolese. Indeed, the local Christians often heard Bwana Mukubwa say, 'If Jesus Christ be God and died for me, then there can be no sacrifice too great for me to make for him.' These words exhorted many of them to sacrifice all for Jesus.

Sadness descended upon Ibambi when the news of Priscilla's unexpected death came the following year. She had been visiting a friend in Spain and suddenly became ill and died. The message, that 'Mama Bwana has gone to be with the Lord Jesus in heaven,' spread

From Cricket to Christ

quickly throughout the region. The local Christians made it a priority to uphold their treasured Bwana Mukubwa in prayer.

Then, in 1930, an officer in Belgian uniform knocked on the bamboo door-frame of C.T.'s hut in Ibambi. He was on government business with a special message for the missionary. The King of the Belgians, Leopold II, was awarding C.T. Studd with the honour of Chevalier of the Royal Order of the Lion, in recognition of his services in the Congo and to the crown of Belgium. It was gratefully received, but the only reward C.T. was truly interested in was the crown of life which God has promised to those who love him, and who remain steadfast under trial.[1]

C.T. Studd was unwavering in the urgent mission of the church to proclaim Jesus Christ to every nation, including those deemed 'unreachable' with the gospel, such as the cannibal tribes of the dense tropical rainforests in the heart of Africa.

A short illness in the summer of 1931 hastened his death. Lying motionless on his bed, C.T. was attended to by colleagues and was surrounded by the African people whom he loved dearly. He did not have the strength to talk; the only audible and distinguishable word from his lips was, 'Hallelujah!' and came forth with every feeble breath he took.

C.T. breathed his last shortly after 10.30 p.m. on Thursday, 16th July 1931.

---

1. See James 1:12.

The sad day of his burial was dampened further by the torrential rain that pelted the mourners and camouflaged the tears on their cheeks. Over two thousand local Christians gathered to pay their last respects to their beloved Bwana Mukubwa.

When the news of his death reached London, Alfred Buxton penned the most fitting tribute of his dear friend and mentor.

> C.T.'s life stands as some rugged Gibraltar – a sign to all succeeding generations that it is worthwhile to lose all this world can offer and stake everything on the world to come. His life will be an eternal rebuke to easy-going Christianity. He has demonstrated what it means to follow Christ without counting the cost and without looking back.[2]

Charles Thomas Studd wholeheartedly surrendered his life to Jesus Christ as Saviour and Lord. He sacrificed so much, that he might tell others of the One who sacrificed his life on a cross for the sins of the whole world.[3]

C.T. was fully convinced, 'If Jesus Christ be God and died for me, then there can be no sacrifice too great for me to make for him.' These words are still the motto of the Worldwide Evangelistic Crusade – the mission he founded all those years ago in the heart of Africa. These words remain a fitting challenge to all Christian people today.

---

2. *Reluctant Missionary,* by Edith Buxton (Hodder and Stoughton, London, 1968) page 178.
3. 1 John 2:2.

C.T. Studd:
Timeline

1860	Charles Thomas Studd born in London, England.
1864	Priscilla Livingstone Stewart born in Lisburn, Northern Ireland.
1877	Edward Studd converted to Christ.
1878	C.T. converted to Christ.
1880	Entered Trinity College Cambridge.
1880-1884	Cricket Career.
1885	Mission to China with Cambridge Seven.
1885	Priscilla converted to Christ.
1887	C.T. gave away his inheritance. Priscilla and C.T. meet in Shanghai, China.
1888	C.T. and Priscilla get married.
1894	The Studds returned to England from China.
1895-1900	C.T. toured Britain and the U.S.A.
1900	Mission in India.
1906	The Studds returned to England from India.
1910	C.T. sailed to Sudan to explore the possibilities of mission in Africa.
1913	Mission to Africa with Alfred Buxton. First base of the Heart of Africa Mission

established in Niangara in the Belgian Congo.

1914 C.T. went back to England to try to recruit more missionaries.

1915 Baptisms in Niangara.

1916 C.T. sailed to Africa with a group of new missionaries, including his daughter Edith Studd.

1917 Edith Studd married Alfred Buxton in Africa.

1918 The Buxtons returned to England from Africa.

1919 Heart of Africa Mission becomes known as the World Evangelization Crusade.

1920 Pauline (nee Studd) and Norman Grubb arrived in the Belgian Congo.

1920 Priscilla Studd recruitment and support tour of U.S.A.

1921 Alfred and Edith Buxton returned to the Congo.

1921 W.E.C. American Council formed.

1922 Headquarters now based at Ibambi in the Ituri Province.

1923 10th Anniversary of the mission to the heart of Africa. Forty missionaries now working in the African mission field.

1925	Due to illness, Alfred and Edith Buxton returned to England.
1928	Priscilla visited C.T in Ibambi – their final meeting.
1929	Priscilla Studd suddenly took ill and died in Spain.
1930	C.T. awarded 'Chevalier of the Royal Order of the Lion' by Leopold II, King of the Belgians, for his services in the Congo and to the crown.
1931	Charles Thomas Studd died and was buried in Ibambi, Belgian Congo.

Thinking Further

Chapter One – A Daring Rescue
The rescuers fought the kidnappers in order to save lives and bring Nancy home. Is there ever a situation where it is necessary to use force in order to restrain evil, bearing in mind that Jesus told his followers to love their enemies? To begin thinking about this, read Romans 12:17 – 13:1-7.

Chapter Two – The Years of Change
Edward Studd heard the gospel of Jesus Christ from a visiting evangelist in London. He repented of his sins and believed. He wanted his family to come to a saving faith in Jesus too. Why did Edward think it was important for his family to know Christ personally? Do you think it's important for people to hear the gospel? Why? Read 1 Timothy 1:12-17 and Luke 19:10.

Chapter Three – A Clear Mind
A tract written by an atheist challenged C.T. deeply. It shook him out of his spiritual lethargy and cleared his mind to action for Christ. Are you concerned about the 'Immortal souls around [you], soon to be everlasting happy or everlasting miserable'? Read Acts 17:30-31.

Chapter Four – The Mission to China

The Cambridge Seven travelled to China to spread the gospel of Jesus Christ. Do you think Christian mission to other countries is vital, or is it arrogant for Christians to think that other religions are wrong? Read Matthew 28:19-20 and Acts 4:12.

Chapter Five – A Great Giveaway

Growing up with privilege in England, C.T. was surrounded by people who believed that riches brought happiness, and they constantly sought to increase their wealth. After his conversion, C.T. gave away his vast fortune in service of Jesus Christ because he felt it was wrong to pursue financial wealth as a servant of Jesus Christ. What do you think? Read Luke 18:18-30, 1 Timothy 6:9-12 and James 1:11.

Chapter Six – Meeting Priscilla

C.T. met Priscilla Livingstone Stewart in Shanghai. When Priscilla finally agreed to marry him, C.T. wrote, 'It is more than enough for me that you are a true child and lover of the Lord Jesus'. If you are a Christian, is it important to you that your future husband or wife is 'a true child and lover of the Lord Jesus'? Read 2 Corinthians 6:14-15.

Chapter Seven – No Foreign Devils Here!

In the early days at Lungan-Fu, the Studds faced persecution and attack from the local population. Why do you think people react badly to the good news about Jesus Christ? Read Jeremiah 17:9, Mark 7:20-23, and John 5:40-43.

Chapter Eight – The Mission to India

The Studd children were baptized at Ooty in India. What is baptism and why is it so important for Christians? Read Mark 1:4-9, Acts 2:38-41, Romans 6:3-4, 1 Corinthians 12:13 and Galatians 3:27 to help you think about this.

Chapter Nine – Cannibals Want Missionaries!

Dr Kumm reported that there was a dire need for the people of Central Africa to hear the gospel about Jesus, but no one had gone there to tell them. Why do you think no one went? Read Psalm 118:6-9 and 1 Peter 3:13-17.

Chapter Ten – Journey to the Heart of Africa

Alfred Buxton was on his way to be a doctor but gave it all up to go to Africa as a missionary with C.T. Studd. Is there anything important to you that you would be prepared to give up in the service of Jesus Christ? Read Mark 10:28-31.

Chapter Eleven – The Mission in Africa

Life in the jungle the was hard for the missionaries. Why would someone leave the comforts of home to live in mud huts in the middle of an African rainforest? How

133

do you think C.T. Studd would answer this question? Would you do it? Read Romans 5:6-11 and Acts 1:8 to get you thinking about this.

Chapter Twelve – Bwana Mukubwa

C.T. Studd preached the gospel to the African people for many years. He translated much of the Scriptures into their languages. Do you think it is important for people to hear and to have the Word of God in their own language? If so, why? Read John 6:68-69 and 2 Timothy 3:16.

OTHER BOOKS IN THE
TRAIL BLAZERS SERIES

Augustine, The Truth Seeker
ISBN 978-1-78191-296-6
John Calvin, After Darkness Light
ISBN 978-1-78191-550-9
Fanny Crosby, The Blind Girl's Song
ISBN 978-1-78191-163-1
Eric Liddell, Finish the Race
ISBN 978-1-84550-590-5
Martin Luther, Reformation Fire
ISBN 978-1-78191-521-9
Robert Moffat, Africa's Brave Heart
ISBN 978-1-84550-715-2
D.L. Moody, One Devoted Man
ISBN 978-1-78191-676-6
Mary of Orange, At the Mercy of Kings
ISBN 978-1-84550-818-0
Patrick of Ireland: The Boy who Forgave
ISBN: 978-1-78191-677-3
Polycarp, Faithful unto Death
ISBN: 978-1-5271-1029-8
John Wycliffe, According to the Word
ISBN 978-1-5271-1080-9
Ulrich Zwingli, Shepherd Warrior
ISBN 978-1-78191-803-6

For a full list of Trail Blazers, please see our
website: www.christianfocus.com

All Trail Blazers are available as e-books

Thomas Clarkson
The Giant With One Idea
by Emily J. Maurits

Thomas Clarkson was the son of a clergyman who lived in a time when it was legal to buy and sell slaves. He believed this was wrong, and campaigned to make sure this changed. He was instrumental in making sure that no human being could be bought or sold in the British Empire.

ISBN: 978-1-5271-0677-2

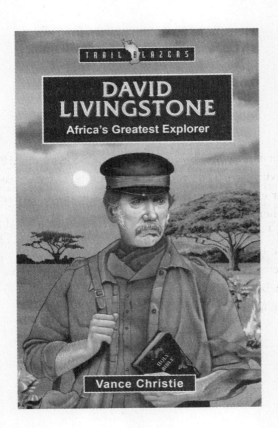

David Livingstone
Africa's Greatest Explorer
by Vance Christie

Born into humble beginnings in Scotland in 1813, Livingstone's life was shaped by his faith and a passion for exploration. Inspired by the Gospel's call to serve others, Livingstone pursued a path of missionary work and exploration, driven by a deep conviction to share the love of Christ with those in distant lands. Despite facing adversity and hardship, he remained steadfast in his belief that God had called him to Africa to spread the message of salvation.

ISBN: 978-1-5271-1163-9

Polycarp
Faithful Unto Death
by David Luckman

Polycarp was Bishop of Smyrna (a city in modern–day Turkey) in the days of the early church. He was a disciple of the apostle John. He was martyred in his eighties for refusing to burn incense to the Roman emperor. David Luckman's new biography in the Trail Blazer series shows readers how this brave man's faith was the most important thing to him.

ISBN: 978-1-5271-1029-8

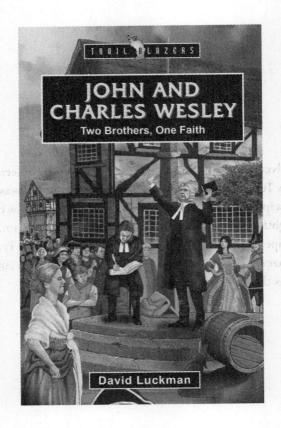

John and Charles Wesley
Two Brothers, One Faith
by David Luckman

Polycarp was Bishop of Smyrna (a city in modern–day Turkey) in the days of the early church. He was a disciple of the apostle John. He was martyred in his eighties for refusing to burn incense to the Roman emperor. David Luckman's new biography in the Trail Blazer series shows readers how this brave man's faith was the most important thing to him.

ISBN: 978-1-5271-1162-2

Christian Focus is for Kids

That means you and your friends can all find a book to help you from the CF4KIDS range – from the very littlest baby to kids that are almost too old to be called a kid anymore.

We publish books that introduce you to the real Jesus, the truth of God's Word, and what that means for boys and girls of all ages.

Reading books is a fun way to find out what it is like to be a follower of Jesus Christ.

True stories, adventures, activity books, and devotions – they are all here for you and your family.

Christian Focus is part of the family of God. We aim to glorify Jesus and help you trust and follow Him.

Christian Focus Publications Ltd,
Geanies House, Fearn, Ross-shire,
IV20 1TW, Scotland,
United Kingdom.
www.christianfocus.com